Other books by Rick Thompson:

Radical Growth:
Five Essentials for Spiritual Vitality

The Long-Expected Jesus:
*How the Old Testament Reveals the Coming
of the Son of God*

The Healthy Church:
Seven Principles Every Member Should Know

The Way of the Cross
A Forty-day Journey

Rick Thompson

Author: Rick Thompson
Editors: Laura A. Long and Sarah Sutton
Graphic Design and Layout: Brad Mardis
Photography: Tallie Thompson

This book is dedicated to my lifelong friends, Mike and Mary Ann Thomas. Never has a pastor been more blessed by faithful friendship than I have by theirs.

Table of Contents

Prologue

Then Jesus was led by the Spirit into the wilderness to be tempted by the devil. After fasting forty days and forty nights, he was hungry. The tempter came to him and said, "If you are the Son of God, tell these stones to become bread." Jesus answered, "It is written: 'Man shall not live on bread alone, but on every word that comes from the mouth of God'" (Matthew 4:1-4).

The fact that you are reading this right now likely means you have made the choice to participate in the Lenten season this year. Maybe you, like me, were raised in a faith tradition that looks suspiciously at this observance. But increasingly, evangelical Christians are shedding those suspicions and discovering the beauty of the Lenten season. The Christian calendar came about because wise spiritual leaders all those years ago came to see the value of focusing their hearts for a time on some of the truly important doctrines of the faith, such as the incarnation at Advent, the atonement during Lent, resurrection during Easter, and ecclesiology at Pentecost. I think they were not wrong.

Lent is a tradition dating back to the Council of Nicaea in 325 A.D. In a culture that no longer values tradition and is obsessed with the here and now, I believe it is more important than ever for the church to strive to put the "holy" back into the holidays. Christmas is meant not only as a day to open presents, but also as a season of reflection. Easter is not simply a day to dress up in new clothes, but an entire season to focus on spiritual matters. Over the years, the church has increasingly lost these seasons to the materialism and commercialism of pop culture. It is time for the church to wrestle them back from secular society and to make them Christian seasons again.

As evangelicals, we distinguish our theology from Catholicism, but that does not mean we should thoughtlessly abolish certain long traditions simply because Catholics have maintained them. I believe God has preserved certain ancient traditions within his church over time to challenge and renew the hearts of his people. Lent is just such a tradition.

The forty days of Lent is a time to focus on the cross, beginning with Ash Wednesday and ending on Good Friday. What can be better than that? The cross is the most important reality that overwhelms every other reality and should be the central focus of every human heart.

Interestingly, forty days carries biblical significance. The number shows up so often in the Bible that many scholars see it as a period of testing, renewal, and life change. The length of time may even have behavioral significance—studies by University College, London, published in the European Journal of Social Psychology (July 2009) found it takes between twenty and sixty days for a person to form new habits. There certainly seems to be some kind of spiritual meaning when we look at the many biblical examples of forty days:

In the Old Testament, when God destroyed the earth with water, He caused it to rain 40 days and 40 nights (Genesis 7:12). Moses was on Mount Sinai for 40 days and 40 nights (Exodus 24:18). Moses interceded on Israel's behalf for 40 days and 40 nights (Deuteronomy 9:18, 25). The Israelite spies took 40 days to spy out Canaan (Numbers 13:25). Goliath taunted Saul's army for 40 days before David arrived to slay him (1 Samuel 17:16). When Elijah fled from Jezebel, he traveled 40 days and 40 nights to Mt. Horeb (1 Kings 19:8). In the New Testament, Jesus was tempted for 40 days and 40 nights (Matthew 4:2). There were 40 days between Jesus' resurrection and ascension (Acts 1:3).

Many people use these forty days this time of year to form helpful new habits or to break harmful ones. I think it is a good idea to apply some kind of healthy discipline to the season whether it involves taking something away or adding something new. Who knows, maybe you will make a great new change that will last a lifetime!

I have written this book to have a devotional focus on the significant events that took place in the forty days leading up to the cross. How do we get forty days between Ash Wednesday and Good Friday when on the calendar that time span is forty-six days? We skip the six Sundays from the fast because they represent Christ's resurrection. We will use those days to reflect on what we have learned through the week.

Each week during Lent, read a chapter a day from Monday to Saturday, and on Sunday take the time to do the reflections. If you are doing this study as a small group, use the Sunday reflection as an overview for the week with a group discussion.

If this is a new journey for you, my hope and prayer is that you will find the Lenten season to be as big of a blessing as it has been to me and my family through the years. Recognizing the seasons of the church calendar has richly blessed my family, and I have written this book to help others experience the richness of this beautiful, ancient church tradition. I am thankful that you are on this journey with me.

Week One: Journey to Bethany

John 11:1–43

Day 1: Courage

So when he heard that Lazarus was sick, Jesus stayed where he was two more days, and then he said to his disciples, "Let us go back to Judea." "But Rabbi," they said, "a short while ago the Jews there tried to stone you, and yet you are going back?"

Then Thomas (also known as Didymus) said to the rest of the disciples, "Let us also go, that we may die with him" (John 11:1–2, 16).

Jesus was a marked man.

In Roman-occupied Israel in the first century, he was increasingly viewed as a possible usurper to the empire. Jewish religious leaders were convinced he was guilty of blasphemy, and they wanted him stopped. Rumors persisted that he talked of a new kingdom—a kingdom that would last forever. At this time in his public ministry, Jesus could go nowhere without huge crowds of admirers shouting his name. The last time Jesus had been in Jerusalem, the situation had almost spiraled out of control, and the disciples undoubtedly felt they had been lucky to make it out alive. Jesus had survived an assassination attempt by religious leaders:

> *"We are not stoning you for any good work," they told him, "but for blasphemy, because you, a mere man, claim to be God!"* (John 10:33)

To put it in modern terms, Jesus' brand had become wildly popular and controversial, and the powers that be were nervous.

All potential insurgents in first-century Judea were on a watch list, and Jesus had captured the attention of the paranoid Roman authorities and their Jewish collaborators. To his followers, he was a beloved messiah, but to Roman and Jewish leaders, he was a growing threat— and threats to Rome's absolute power were highly likely to be smashed like bugs. The disciples knew all too well that the Romans didn't mess around when it came to sending a message.

So when Jesus told his nervous band of followers that

he intended to go to Bethany, a stone's throw from the political and religious hot seat of Jerusalem, the disciples had no illusions about where Jesus was taking them or his intentions. They would be returning to the center of controversy, and thus, dangerously close to the very authorities who wanted to silence Jesus. Thomas verbalized what they all must have been thinking, "Let us also go, that we may die with him."

It turns out, Thomas' fears were valid. A short time after he uttered those words, Jesus was arrested and crucified on a Roman cross outside Jerusalem.

The Latin word for torture is *"crucifix,"* which literally means "fixed to a beam." With years of experience stamping out insurrections, the Romans had perfected many forms of torture and execution to make a lasting impression on subject states—strangling, stoning, burning, and even boiling in oil. But nailing a prisoner to a beam sent a more lingering message and had become a staple in the Roman Empire. New Testament scholar Hal Taussig wrote:

> *Romans practiced both random and intentional violence against populations they had conquered, killing tens of thousands by crucifixion.* ("How Romans Used Crucifixion as a Political Weapon," *Newsweek Magazine*, April, 2015)

No wonder that after many years of this brutal form of execution, the very Latin word for torture became associated with crucifixion! The Latin word for cross, crux, has crept into the English language in words such as excruciating, critical, cruel, and crisis. When we say we are getting to the "crux of the matter," we mean we are focusing on the biggest struggle of the decision. The memory of the Roman cross is embedded in our language.

And Jesus accepted that fate purposefully. The Jewish leaders who orchestrated his arrest may have thought they had carefully planned his capture on the Mount of Olives, but Jesus already had made the first move when he told the disciples, "Let us go to Judea."

Jesus and the disciples were in a safe zone on the other side of the Jordan, in the land known as the Decapolis. Distanced from Judea and the strongholds of political power and religious fervor, they were practically unnoticed. The disciples could see the unfolding controversy surrounding Jesus and knew they needed to lie low and stay out of trouble.

But the world is not transformed by people who stay in safe zones. Clearly, Jesus had chosen his path carefully. The Roman authorities may have considered Jesus as just another insurgent to hang on a cross, but in truth, they were playing into his hands. Consider the choices

Jesus made in the days before his entry into Jerusalem:

- He waited two days before deciding to go to Judea when he learned Lazarus was sick, long enough for Lazarus to die. (Raising a dead man gets more headlines.)

- He crossed the Jordan and traveled directly to Judea and into Bethany, drawing a huge crowd just a few miles from the Jewish temple and the seat of Roman power at the Antonia fortress.

- He dramatically confirmed his authenticity as the Messiah by raising a man from the grave.

So much for lying low and not drawing much attention.

The news of Lazarus' healing must have spread like wildfire throughout Jerusalem and Judea. If the Jewish and Roman authorities had any qualms about Jesus' popularity before this event, they certainly had reason to fear it now! Most people think of the raising of Lazarus as just another of Jesus' many miracles, but the act also was his first dramatic step toward eventual arrest, crucifixion, and resurrection. In that context, the miracle was profoundly provocative—like pouring gasoline on a raging fire. Jesus had work to accomplish, which involved his sacrificial death on a cruel cross. His trip to Bethany sent an unmistakable signal to Jerusalem. He was stirring up the fears of the Romans and the Sanhedrin. He was daring to kick the hornets' nest.

And the disciples knew it.

Crossing the Jordan to Judea meant taking Thomas and the disciples out of their safe zone—from safety to danger, from anonymity to controversy—and toward the most consequential, excruciating event in human history.

We can draw some important lessons from the act of crossing the Jordan. To make significant progress in life, we will frequently need to have the courage to get out of our safe zone and cross over into uncertainty. Such an action is, in fact, one of the most important themes of the Old Testament. When the Israelites were liberated from the bondage of Egypt, they were directed to move boldly into the land of Canaan, the land of promise. The land was beautiful, abundant, and promised to them by God, but there were giants in the land. To claim God's promises, the Israelites had to be willing to cross the Jordan and face the dreaded Canaanites in battle.

The Lord God gave these instructions to Joshua as he prepared to lead them across:

"Be strong and courageous, because you'll be leading this people to inherit the land that I promised to give their ancestors. Only be strong and very courageous to ensure that you obey all the instructions that my servant Moses gave you—turn neither to the right nor to the left from it—so that you may succeed wherever you go. This set of instructions is not to cease being a part of your conversations. Meditate on it day and night, so that you may be careful to carry out everything that's written in it, for then you'll prosper and succeed. I've commanded you, haven't I? Be strong and courageous. Don't be fearful or discouraged, because the LORD your God is with you wherever you go." Then Joshua gave orders to the officials of the people. "Go through the camp," he said, "and command the people, 'Prepare provisions for yourselves, because within three days you'll be crossing the Jordan River to take possession of the land that the LORD your God is giving you—so go get it!'" (Joshua 1:6–11 ISV)

God's instructions to the Israelites thousands of years ago are as relevant to us as if they were written this morning. There is a promised land in front of us, but we must be willing to face our fear, get out of our safe zone, and cross over into uncertainty. We must be strong and courageous, not fearful or discouraged. Promised lands are preceded by Jordan crossings. As I look back on my life, I can see clearly that the times of most significant and important progress were those when I broke free from the comfortable and moved toward the unknown and less secure.

What was true for the Israelites moving into the land of promise was also true for the Lord Jesus and the disciples that day in the Decapolis. The way of the cross leads to a new and better promised land. But we must have the courage to cross the Jordan.

Day Two: Choices

*Then Thomas (also known as Didymus) said
to the rest of the disciples, "Let us also go,
that we may die with him"* (John 11:16).

Today is a day of decision for you. Your decision to
pick up this book and plunge into devotional thought is
a good start, a solid choice. What happens in your life
from here will be determined by the subsequent choices
you make from this day forward.

To a large degree you are a product of your choices.
The decisions you have made in the past have set you
on a course resulting in the person you have become.
The choice of who or whether to marry, where to live,
your career, your home, your diet, your friendships, and
the thousands of seemingly inconsequential choices
in between are woven together to form the fabric of
your life, making you who you are today. Ralph Waldo
Emerson once famously said:

Sow a thought and you reap an action;

Sow an act and you reap a habit;

Sow a habit and you reap a character;

Sow a character and you reap a destiny.

The Bible teaches that God has created in us an amazing quality from his image—the ability to make choices, and therefore, to play our part in shaping our destiny. One of the questions I am often asked as a pastor is whether human beings have free will, or is all of life predetermined by God? The answer to the question is yes! The Bible is clear that both are true simultaneously. That may seem completely contradictory and irreconcilable, like oil and water or light and darkness, and yet the Bible teaches both. We choose our path and then God redeems our choices. This concept has such intellectual complexity that we find it difficult to embrace. And yet the Bible teaches it over and again. Proverbs 16:9 says:

In his heart a man plans his course, but the Lord determines his steps.

What can this possibly mean? It means our plans are our plans, our choices are our choices, and we are responsible for them. No one forces us to make our choices. God does not decide for us or choose our direction. If we do something stupid, wicked, or cruel, we are totally and completely responsible for our actions, and we suffer the consequences. We alone are held accountable for the choices we make.

Judas made his own tragic choice to betray Jesus and paid the consequences, and yet his choice of betrayal simultaneously fit into God's providential plan to lead Jesus to arrest and the cross.

Our plans are ours, but in a historical and eternal sense, the actual results of those plans are completely and totally under the sovereign will of God. Nothing happens that is not according to his plan. Both our free will and God's sovereign plan are true at the same time.

The balance of this biblical teaching is important to how we live. If we tilt our hearts too far in either direction, we end up in the wrong place. If we live as if there is no direction from God's sovereign will, our hearts will inevitably fall into despair at the prospect of a meaningless universe. On the other hand, if we believe that nothing we think, say, or do really matters because God has predetermined everything, we will see no reason to get up in the morning.

The Bible teaches that both free will and God's sovereignty are important to the human heart. God is in control. Our choices make a difference. Both are true.

Consider the monumental choices that have impacted our world. What would our lives be like today if Gutenberg had not invented the printing press or Bell the telephone? What if the Wright brothers had not chosen to turn a bicycle into a flying machine, or if Ford had not decided to dedicate his life to the horseless carriage called an automobile? What if Edison had not chosen to harness the power of electricity to produce light, or if Steve Jobs had not innovated computer technology to the size of a billfold? Think of how the world would be different if Steven Werner Lee had not invented the World Wide Web?

One of the greatest powers in the universe is the power to choose.

Famed psychiatrist Victor Frankl was a survivor of the horrors of the Auschwitz concentration camp in Nazi Germany in the 1940s. He later recounted his experiences in the book, *Man's Search for Meaning* (1959). In this amazing autobiography, Frankl made the observation that his Nazi captors could take away everything he held dear in his life except for one thing—the power to choose:

We who lived in concentration camps can

remember the men who walked through the huts comforting others, giving away their last piece of bread. They may have been few in number, but they offered sufficient proof that everything can be taken from a man but one thing: the last of the human freedoms—to choose one's attitude in any given set of circumstances, to choose one's own way.

Thomas made a fateful choice: "Let us go with him to die." It was a choice to follow the Savior, no matter the cost. A courageous choice. A choice to follow him wherever that would lead, no matter the dangers or sorrows ahead. The old hymn written by Earnest Blandy in 1890 could have been written for Thomas:

Where he leads me I will follow.
I'll go with him through the waters.
I'll go with him through the garden.
I'll go with him to dark Calvary.
I'll go with him through the judgment.
He will lead me to grace and glory.
I'll go with him, with him, all the way.

Thomas made his choice and followed Jesus all the way to Jerusalem and to crucifixion. After the resurrection, Thomas alone put his hands on the Savior's wounds, as Jesus said to him:

Because you have seen me, you have believed; blessed are those who have not seen and yet have believed (John 20:29).

Think of all that Thomas experienced in that moment. Jesus Christ, the second part of the Trinity in all his splendid resurrected glory standing directly in front of him, addressing him by name and inviting him to touch his wounds. It must have taken all of Thomas's emotional strength to keep his composure as he felt the Lord's side and his hands. I cannot think of a more unbelievably awesome experience as that!

And yet Jesus said those who don't see and yet believe are even more blessed, a statement that only can mean that the most powerful, stupendous choice any of us will ever make is the choice to believe in the resurrected Jesus: the choice to believe that the God of the universe was wounded for our transgressions, died in our place on a Roman cross, and lives today.

Today and every day is a day of decision. Like Thomas we must decide if we are willing to follow Jesus all the way to the cross. Thomas made the choice—"Let us go and die with him"—and ended up standing face to face with the resurrected Christ in all his glory. Such was God's providential plan for

Thomas. And with the courage to decide, Thomas shaped his destiny.

Day Three: Perspective

When Martha heard that Jesus was coming, she went out to meet him, but Mary stayed at home. "Lord," Martha said to Jesus, "if you had been here, my brother would not have died. But I know that even now God will give you whatever you ask." Jesus said to her, "Your brother will rise again." Martha answered, "I know he will rise again in the resurrection at the last day." Jesus said to her, "I am the resurrection and the life. The one who believes in me will live, even though they die; and whoever lives by believing in me will never die. Do you believe this?" Yes, Lord," she replied, "I believe that you are the Messiah, the Son of God, who is to come into the world."

When Mary reached the place where Jesus was and saw him, she fell at his feet and said, "Lord, if you had been here, my brother

would not have died." When Jesus saw her
weeping, and the Jews who had come along
with her also weeping, he was deeply moved
in spirit and troubled. "Where have you laid
him?" he asked. "Come and see, Lord," they
replied. Jesus wept (John 11:17–35).

Martha and Mary seemed disappointed with Jesus.
Maybe even angry. When Jesus arrived in Bethany, both
the sisters made the same observation: if only Jesus had
been there, Lazarus would not have died. I think all of us
are guilty of the "if only" trap from time to time.

If only I could get that new job...
If only I could find someone to marry...
If only I could get through college...
If only I could make more money...
If only we could have kids...

Some people seem to spend their whole lives saying,
"If only, if only, if only!"

The truth is some of you who are reading this are disappointed with God. Like Mary and Martha you have
started down the "if only" path toward rationalizing your
struggles. Maybe you have lost a loved one, or your
health has been in decline, or a relationship or a job has

gone badly for you. Maybe life is just disappointing in general. Life has become difficult, and you thought that loving Jesus was supposed to anesthetize you from the pain. "Where are you Jesus!" you may be saying.

Many years ago a woman approached the famous pastor, Dr. R. G. Lee, after one of his sermons and asked, "Dr. Lee, where was God when my son was killed in a tragic accident?" Dr. Lee sympathetically replied, "He was in the same place as when his own son died tragically—he was on his throne."

In heaven there are no unanswered questions, only answers. In the scope of eternity, all of our hurts, suffering, and failures will be reconciled into the beauty of God's providential design. No matter how hard life gets, we can rest in the knowledge that God is on his throne. C. S. Lewis once observed that when we get to heaven someday the first word we will say will be, "Aha!" In eternity, everything finally will make sense. Here is what the Bible says:

> *And we know that in all things God works for the good of those who love him, who have been called according to his purpose* (Romans 8:28).

Here is an important truth to understand in the midst of suffering:

God is more interested in your character than he is in your circumstance.

God is in the character-shaping business to prepare us for eternity. From the perspective of eternity, our suffering looks different. I remember years ago Teri and I toured a facility in Turkey where skilled craftsmen were weaving Turkish rugs. Walking into the building, I saw a huge display of rugs hanging from hooks suspended from the ceiling. The rugs looked colorless and unfinished, and I was somewhat surprised that these rugs could be for sale. I soon realized that we had come in the back way and were viewing the rugs from behind.

When I turned around to see the other side of the suspended rugs, their immaculate beauty was in full display, the colors and the designs from the carefully woven threads exploding into view. On the backside of the rug, that beauty was concealed. That experience is a pretty good analogy for our perspective in this life as compared to eternity. On this side of eternity, life often looks dark, confused, and out of sorts, but in the scope of eternity, God is weaving something beautiful and amazing.

Many circumstances in life may perplex and frustrate you. Perhaps you believe God should always rescue you from your pain. You may ask for him to help, cry out to him, plead with him, and bargain with him, and yet God seems to be silent as you fall headlong into your suffering. What has happened? Has God abandoned you? Like Mary and Martha, you might say, "If only you would have been here, Jesus."

But God is weaving a beautiful tapestry from your life that someday will be in full display in eternity. He is not as interested in your circumstances as he is in your character. James 1:2–4 says:

> *Consider it pure joy, my brothers and sisters, whenever you face trials of many kinds, because you know that the testing of your faith produces perseverance. Let perseverance finish its work so that you may be mature and complete, not lacking anything* (James 1:2–4).

All Christians for all time know how the story of Lazarus ended, how it all worked out beautifully for God's glory. But at the time, the two sisters could not have known. They were hurt, grieving, and disappointed with Jesus. If we could see our suffering from God's perspective, we would have a much wider view—the one of eternity. In light of this truth, I have learned to pray a simple prayer:

> *Lord God, give me those things I would ask for if I knew what you know!*

That is a much more productive prayer than the "if only" prayer, which leads to frustration and disappointment, and sometimes even anger or depression. How much better to think of our problems as threads God uses to weave masterpieces in eternity:

> *For we are God's handiwork, created in Christ Jesus to do good works, which God prepared in advance for us to do* (Ephesians 2:10).

I find it interesting how Jesus dealt with the sisters' "if only" questions. They both made the same observation, but his response to each could not have been more different. When Martha observed, "If only you would have been here," Jesus famously taught her a lesson on the resurrection:

> *I am the resurrection and the life. The one who believes in me will live, even though they die* (v. 25).

But when Mary made the very same observation, Jesus said nothing to her. He simply wept.

Jesus' different responses demonstrate two very important aspects of how God confronts our questions. Sometimes he goes for the mind, other times for the heart. Martha needed a theological lesson, but Mary simply needed someone to weep with her. At times we need a lesson, and at other times we need to know that God is with us, empathizing with our tears.

There are times when we should let our questions lead us into the depths of theological truth and better under-standing. And then there are times when we should allow our questions to lead us into a deeper, more intimate relationship with the one who loved us so much he was willing to die in our place. Sometimes we hear his expla-nation; other times we feel his tears.

Day Four: Death

*Then the Jews said, "See how he loved him!"
But some of them said, "Could not he who
opened the eyes of the blind man have kept
this man from dying?" Jesus, once more
deeply moved, came to the tomb. It was a
cave with a stone laid across the entrance.
"Take away the stone," he said. "But, Lord,"
said Martha, the sister of the dead man, "by
this time there is a bad odor, for he has been
there four days." Then Jesus said, "Did I not
tell you that if you believe, you will see the
glory of God?" So they took away the stone.
Then Jesus looked up and said, "Father, I
thank you that you have heard me. I knew
that you always hear me, but I said this for
the benefit of the people standing here, that
they may believe that you sent me." When he
had said this, Jesus called in a loud voice,
"Lazarus, come out!" The dead man came
out, his hands and feet wrapped with strips of*

linen, and a cloth around his face. Jesus said to them, "Take off the grave clothes and let him go" (John 11:34–43).

I have seen death close up. I remember as a young pastor walking into an emergency room with a family whose husband and father had just suffered a heart attack. At that moment, the doctor and nurses pronounced the man dead.

A family I loved was thrown unexpectedly into the pit of despair that day, and I will never forget their crying out, their tears, their anguish. As a pastor, this was my first close experience with death, but there would be many more like it. One of the privileges and anguishes of being a pastor is to walk with families through the shadow of death.

The shadow has passed over me as well. My mother-in-law died very young, when our children were just babies. She would not see her grandkids grow up or enjoy retirement. We were at her bedside when she took her final breath, and I remember looking at her lifeless body and thinking how unnatural it seemed. She had been a spiritual bulwark in our lives and now she was gone. I have no words to describe the hurt I felt at that moment, a pain unmatched until I watched my father struggle for his final breath a few years ago. A man I loved deeply lay before me, lifeless. Even as I write these words I can feel the sense of despair in those moments.

Mary and Martha must have felt that same despair when their brother died. Jesus came to them and comforted them in their grief and cried with them. And then the Bible says something very interesting that is lost in modern translations. In the New International Version (NIV), it sounds very polite and is easy to miss:

Jesus, once more deeply moved...

The original language is much different than this translation. The word translated as "deeply moved" in English is embrimōmenos in Greek, a very difficult word for translators because it directly and literally means something like rage, or "deep seething anger." Perhaps the translators of the NIV were being polite when they used "deeply moved" to communicate Jesus' feelings, because the original language seems to indicate Jesus experienced raging anger.

What are we to make of this? What was going on that would cause Jesus to suddenly feel rage? We know that Jesus had prior knowledge that Lazarus had died because he had already explained the situation to the disciples, so why was he suddenly in a rage? What happened in this moment as Jesus was standing before the grave that would cause him to feel such deep anger?

The only answer seems to be that Jesus was viewing the scandal of death from the perspective of the author of life. The creator of life is deeply infuriated by the presence of death.

Death is an insult to the one who brings life. We read in Genesis 3 that the result of the fall was the deteriorating effects of our sinful rebellion against God. From that moment forward, everything in life began falling apart. Our relationship to God began falling apart as our relationship to others fell apart. Humankind experienced emotional turmoil and began falling apart physically and in every other way.

A good description of death is perpetual separation. Relational death is separation from others, and spiritual death is separation from God. What is emotional death but separation from reality? In physical death, cells separate from one another. Hell itself is eternal separation from God—everlasting death. And all of it came about as a result of the fall in the garden.

But after the fall, God prophesied about the one who would come and reverse the curse and crush the head of the enemy.

When we think of Jesus standing before that grave that day in Bethany, let us see him within the context of Genesis 3. As he looks into the face of death, he is enraged by its effects on his creation. He has come into the world to reverse death's curse and crush the head of the enemy, and here he stands looking right into the pit of death. The rage he feels is the righteous anger of a God who has come to settle the score. The Apostle Paul later wrote:

> *Where, O death, is your victory? Where, O death, is your sting? The sting of death is sin, and the power of sin is the law. But thanks be to God! He gives us the victory through our Lord Jesus Christ* (1 Corinthians 15:55–56).

Jesus sent a dramatic message to those gathered at Mary and Martha's house and to all believers through time. He did not allow death to have the victory over Lazarus; he took away its sting. And that is what he has done for each of us. For my mother-in-law, my father, and for all those who have gone before us who have life in Christ.

He raised Lazarus from the dead, and then told those gathered around to remove his grave clothes and let him go.

The important lesson in these final instructions from Jesus is this: Once you have been given new life in Christ, the grave clothes must go. There is no reason for you to remain in bondage to your former life—the old is gone, the new has come. You are a new creation in Christ Jesus! (2 Corinthians 5:17) The spirit of God living in you will reverse the detrimental effects of old patterns in your life. His life in you will restore relationships and bring health, life, and emotional strength.

With new life in Christ, a new administration takes over, and his spirit manifests new fruit: love, joy, peace, patience, kindness, goodness, faithfulness, gentleness, and self-control. You no longer need to wear the grave clothes of doubt, fear, and anxiousness. It may not happen right away, and you will need others' help to remove them, but slowly the grave clothes will be unbound, and you will be set free.

> *It is for freedom that Christ has set us free. Stand firm, then, and do not let yourselves be burdened again by a yoke of slavery* (Galatians 5:1).

Perhaps today as you continue your journey on the way to the cross, you need to hear Jesus say to you, "Take off the grave clothes! You don't need them anymore. You've been set free. And when I set you free, you are free indeed!"

Sunday Reflection:
Journey to Bethany

Read John 11:1–27.

1. The Decapolis across the Jordan River was a different jurisdiction than Judea, and therefore, the disciples were safer there. Why do you think Thomas and the other disciples would feel more secure in that place?

2. How do we distinguish between playing things safe and courageously following God's lead?

3. In what ways does the Bible illustrate crossing the Jordan? What is to be learned from them. (Read Joshua 1)

4. Why did Jesus delay going into Bethany for two days?

Read John 11:28–44.

5. What statement did Mary and Martha make to Jesus that was exactly the same?

6. How did Jesus respond to them differently? Why do you think he did this?

7. What kind of excitement did the raising of Lazarus cause?

8. What does the miracle of raising Lazarus say to us about the intentions of Jesus the final week?

Week Two: Entry to Jerusalem

Mark 11:1–33

Day 5: Humility

As they approached Jerusalem and came to Bethphage and Bethany at the Mount of Olives, Jesus sent two of his disciples, saying to them, "Go to the village ahead of you, and just as you enter it, you will find a colt tied there, which no one has ever ridden. Untie it and bring it here. If anyone asks you, 'Why are you doing this?' say, 'The Lord needs it and will send it back here shortly.'" They went and found a colt outside in the street, tied at a doorway. As they untied it, some people standing there asked, "What are you doing, untying that colt?" They answered as Jesus had told them to, and the people let them go.

When they brought the colt to Jesus and threw their cloaks over it, he sat on it. Many people spread their cloaks on the road, while others spread branches they had cut in the fields. Those who went ahead and those who followed shouted, "Hosanna! Blessed is he who comes in the name of the Lord! Blessed is the coming kingdom of our father David! Hosanna in the highest heaven!"

Jesus entered Jerusalem and went into the temple courts. He looked around at everything, but since it was already late, he went out to Bethany with the Twelve (Mark 11:1–11).

Let's address the obvious as we consider the triumphal entry of Jesus into Jerusalem: Kings making triumphal entries do not ride on donkeys.

Have you ever seen a full-grown man ride a donkey? I once rode a donkey to the top of Petra in Jordan and my feet dragged the ground all the way up. My wife was in tears from laughter the whole time. The donkey almost got both of us killed at one point by getting too close to a cliff face. I wondered why I wasn't carrying the beast of burden myself.

Children or maybe hobbits ride donkeys, but not kings. Can you imagine Alexander the Great riding into Gaza bouncing awkwardly through the streets on a donkey? Or Cyrus into Babylon? Or how about Caesar into Rome?

No. Not gonna happen. I don't care who you are, you don't look like a conqueror when you are on a donkey.

And that was the point.

Jesus was sending a message that the kingdom he was establishing for all time was a different kind of kingdom. He entered Jerusalem as a servant, the one who would lay down his life for the sins of the world. He did not come as a conquering general to take over kingdoms by force, but as the one to conquer our hearts by his willing submission to the Roman cross.

Zechariah prophesied about this day:

> *Rejoice greatly, Daughter Zion! Shout, Daughter Jerusalem! See, your king comes to you, righteous and victorious, lowly and riding on a donkey, on a colt, the foal of a donkey* (Zechariah 9:9).

Everything about the life of Jesus was surprising and unexpected. God who became flesh was not born as a military hero, a wealthy aristocrat, or politician. He was born in an animal trough to a young mother from a poor family under scandalous circumstances. He spent his childhood in Nazareth, a humble backwater village in the backwater region of Galilee, in the backwater state of Israel in the Roman Empire.

Clearly, God's message to us is his intention to reach into every human heart. No one is excluded from his redemptive intent, no matter how poor or marginalized or low born. The Gospel is accessible to all.

The circumstances of Jesus' life also teach us something else that is vital to the Christian experience: to find life, we have to be willing to humble ourselves. Death to self is the salvific key to slaying our idolatrous nature. Until we lay down our lives, we will not know the meaning of his salvation. Humility is what brings us into life in Christ, and it is the basis for all human relationships. The Apostle Paul says this:

> *In your relationships with one another, have the same mindset as Christ Jesus: Who, being in very nature God, did not consider equality with God something to be used to his own advantage; rather, he made himself nothing by taking the very nature of a servant, being made in human likeness. And being found in appearance as a man, he humbled himself by becoming obedient to death—even death on a cross! Therefore, God exalted him to the highest place and gave him the name that is above every name, that at the*

name of Jesus every knee should bow, in heaven and on earth and under the earth, and every tongue acknowledge that Jesus Christ is Lord, to the glory of God the Father (Philippians 2:5–11).

Many people think humility means to think badly of ourselves, but that is not humility at all! Humility is not thinking less of ourselves, but thinking of ourselves less. In other words, a truly humble person is someone who has enough strength of character to avoid constantly obsessing with self. In his book, *Mere Christianity*, C. S. Lewis digs deeper into this truth:

> *Do not imagine that if you meet a really humble man he will be what most people call "humble" nowadays: he will not be a sort of greasy, smarmy person, who is always telling you that, of course, he is nobody. Probably all you will think about him is that he seemed a cheerful, intelligent chap who took a real interest in what you said to him. If you do dislike him it will be because you feel a little envious of anyone who seems to enjoy life so easily. He will not be thinking about humility: he will not be thinking about himself at all. If anyone would like to acquire humility, I can, I think, tell him the first step. The first step is to*

realize that one is proud. And a biggish step, too. At least, nothing whatever can be done before it. If you think you are not conceited, it means you are very conceited indeed.

When Jesus rode into Jerusalem on a donkey, he demonstrated to all of humanity for all time that his kingdom would stand against the world's kingdoms, which are about self, power, control, wealth, and status. In sharp contrast, the kingdom of God is about humility, love, forgiveness, justice, peace, hope, joy, and serving others.

Jesus said:

> *Even as the Son of Man came not to be served but to serve, and to give his life as a ransom for many* (Matthew 20:28).

The humility of Christ contains awesome power and strength. In John's vision of Christ in Revelation 5, Jesus appears simultaneously as the Lion of Judah and the Lamb that was slain—both God incarnate and the suffering servant, two seemingly irreconcilable identities. In John's account of the Last Supper, he makes a remarkable observation about the nature of Christ:

Jesus knew that the Father had put all things under his power, and that he had come from God and was returning to God; so he got up from the meal, took off his outer clothing, and wrapped a towel around his waist. After that, he poured water into a basin and began to wash his disciples' feet, drying them with the towel (John 13:2–5).

Jesus knew that he had all things under his power and that he had come from God and was returning to God, and so what did he do? He washed feet—dirty, disgusting feet that had been in sandals on dusty roads laden with animal dung and worse. The job of washing feet was usually given to the lowliest household servant. But there he was, the God of the universe become flesh, putting a towel around his waist and washing feet.

The way of the cross is the way of humility. It is a journey of denying self, which I believe is singularly important for finding joy in relationships. Pride destroys relationships, but humility gives them life.

How does one grow in humility? We have to allow Jesus to control our thoughts and attitudes. The spirit of Christ has to grow in us:

Let the Spirit change your way of thinking and make you into a new person (Ephesians 4:23–24 CEV).

The truth is we become like the people with whom we spend time. If we spend time with negative people, we become negative. If we spend time with encouraging people, we become more encouraging. If you want to have more humility, spend time with Jesus Christ. Study his word, talk to him in prayer, and follow his path. Jesus' life was characterized by humility and servanthood. His path leads to washing dirty feet when it's the servants job and riding donkeys when everyone expects a war horse. It's about thinking less of self. It is the path to the cross.

But it is also the path to life and hope and glorious resurrection.

Day 6: Transformation

The next day as they were leaving Bethany, Jesus was hungry. Seeing in the distance a fig tree in leaf, he went to find out if it had any fruit. When he reached it, he found nothing but leaves, because it was not the season for figs. Then he said to the tree, "May no one ever eat fruit from you again." And his disciples heard him say it (Mark 11:12–14).

Our Scripture today is one of the most bizarre stories in all the Gospels. When we read this passage, the natural question is, "What does Jesus have against fig trees?" The story sounds like completely irrational aggression against an innocent plant. Why would Jesus be angry at a non-producing fig tree that isn't even in season? The tree was just beginning to leaf, and fully ripened figs were weeks away. What is up with Jesus' actions toward this poor plant?

In reality, Jesus is not dealing with a fig tree in this story; he's dealing with us. He's getting in our faces. The story is really about the human condition.

First, when figs were not in season, travelers often enjoyed the buds of a leafing fig tree, which were as tasty and nutritious as the fruit itself. A fig tree with no buds while in leaf was obviously diseased and already dying. So Jesus was simply stating reality: On the outside, the tree appeared to be able to bear fruit, but on the inside, it was dead and nonproductive.

Second, the story has a meaning beyond the literal desire to enjoy fruit. The true meaning comes alive when we consider the context. The story, situated between Jesus' two visits to Jerusalem and the temple, is a parable about people caught up in religious activity, but who have no true relationship with God. Jesus was imparting a lesson about looking good on the outside but being dead on the inside.

Think about what Jesus encountered at the temple: people who were busy with religious activity, and yet their hearts were far from God. A genuine relationship with the living God should produce living fruit in the life of the follower. True worship should result in spiritual transformation.

The operative question for every believer is, "Has my life been radically changed by God's spirit living in me? Is my life bearing fruit, or am I just going through the motions of religious activity?"

If you are an angry person, have you overcome your anger?

If you tend to have a hard heart, is your heart softening as the spirit works in you?

If you are a fearful person or a jealous person or a person who tends to be negative, has your life changed to the degree that those around you can see spiritual transformation?

If not, you might want to think about the lesson of the fig tree.

Day 7: Cleanliness

Jesus entered the temple courts and drove out all who were buying and selling there. He overturned the tables of the money changers and the benches of those selling doves. "It is written," he said to them, " 'My house will be called a house of prayer,' but you are making it 'a den of robbers'" (Matthew 22:12–13).

Do you not know that you are God's temple and that God's Spirit dwells in you? (1 Corinthians 10:13)

Saturday morning was always for housecleaning when I was growing up. Both of my parents worked during the week, so my brothers and I pretty much had free reign of the place Monday through Friday. We tended to leave clothes where we shed them, and our bathroom was a mess.

Our working mom did not have the time or the emotional

tenacity to follow us around and continually clean up after us during weekdays, but on Saturday, the chickens came home to roost. Saturday was cleaning day. I vividly remember waking up to the roar of a vacuum cleaner and the odor of detergents and polishes—the sounds and smells of Saturday morning. I remember with a sense of dread what it was like to face my mother's determined will. She put on her serious face, and with backup from Dad, neither cartoons, street baseball games, unfinished tree houses, nor life, nor death, nor angel, nor demon, nor any other living creature could prevent us from participating in the housecleaning.

On Saturdays we were reminded that Mom was in charge, and she was rising up to regain control of the house and give it a thorough cleaning. And all of us kids fell right in line to the force of her authority.

I remember wondering as a kid why Mom was so obsessed with things being clean. What did it matter? Why wash clothes? They will just get dirty again. Why clean a room only to see it fall back into disorder? Wouldn't it be better to just chill out on Saturdays and save the cleaning for when we really need it, like holidays and blue moons?

And then I moved off to college and lived with a bunch of college guys for a semester and learned firsthand what happens to kitchens and bathrooms when you don't clean them for several weeks. Things begin to smell bad, and strange bacteria begin to grow in unexpected places. My buddies and I seemed to be always getting sick, and our clothes certainly weren't cleaning themselves. It slowly dawned on me that when you let things follow their natural course, they will go down a path of destruction and chaos.

I found the explanation in my physics class when the professor explained the law of entropy: Everything in the universe is separating into different systems and falling apart. I immediately thought of my apartment and especially my one roommate who ate a lot of peanut butter and honey and let the dishes pile up in the sink.

My mom quoted the oft-used phrase, "Cleanliness is next to godliness," as if it were Scripture. In fact, I was in seminary before I realized that statement wasn't in the Bible! She never said any different. She knew that a clean home was a healthy home. She knew that without regular periods of cleaning house, she would lose the battle to entropy.

What is true for our homes is also true for the spiritual life. The Bible teaches we are all fallen and our nature is in disrepair, and unless we take seriously our need for confession and cleansing and begin to tend to our souls, the dishes will start piling up and things will begin smelling bad.

David is described in the Bible as a man "after God's own heart." He was the anointed one, the beloved King of Israel whose lineage would bring about the Messiah. And yet for all of David's righteous deeds and regular praise to God, he let his spiritual life entropy. He became a mess. His life fell into a cycle of sin and despair and finally repentance and restoration. In other words, David was just like us. His most famous confession is found in Psalm 51:

> *Create in me a pure heart, O God,*
> *and renew a steadfast spirit within me.*
> *Do not cast me from your presence*
> *or take your Holy Spirit from me.*
> *Restore to me the joy of your salvation*
> *and grant me a willing spirit, to sustain me.*

On his way to the cross, Jesus stopped by the temple to give it a good cleansing. No doubt he was making a statement about his authority. No doubt he was making a serious point about injustice, religious hypocrisy, and greed. And by offending the religious and political authorities who controlled his fate, he also cast the die for his arrest and crucifixion.

But I believe Jesus also wanted to make the point that all temples need a good housecleaning now and then.

Day 8: Will

On reaching Jerusalem, Jesus entered the temple courts and began driving out those who were buying and selling there. He overturned the tables of the money changers and the benches of those selling doves, and would not allow anyone to carry merchandise through the temple courts. And as he taught them, he said, "Is it not written: 'My house will be called a house of prayer for all nations'? But you have made it 'a den of robbers'" (Mark 11:15–17).

The story of Jesus cleansing the temple reminds me of my Saturday mornings as a kid. To some it may seem odd or even impossible that one man could take over a space so vast, and single handedly wreak havoc on hundreds of market stalls in the crowded temple courtyard a few days before the Passover meal. According to the historian, Josephus, it was not unusual for more than

400,000 animals to be sold in that courtyard on the week of Passover. That's a lot of table turning! But people who doubt it could happen must not have had a mom like mine. When it came to Saturday housecleaning, she had the will, the moral authority, and the power. Nothing was stopping her.

And those were exactly the same qualities that Jesus possessed as he walked into the temple courts on the way to the cross and cleaned his father's house, except that he had them on a divine scale.

No doubt Jesus was not the first person to notice that things were out of control at the temple. There had to have been many who loved the law and understood that the temple was to be a place of worship and reverence for almighty God. And yet making real change that sends a clear message about what is important requires the willpower and emotional fortitude.

Picture this scene: Jesus walks in through the temple's outer gate and stands in the outer courtyard, the Court of the Gentiles. Perhaps the Jews thought that if Gentiles were allowed to be there, anything was permissible, and so they filled the courtyard with just about everything you can imagine.

In those days, the space was known as the "Bazaar

of Annas," named for the high priest, a corrupt, greedy man who viewed the temple as a vehicle to attain power and wealth. Annas and his priests sold concessions to merchants who could occupy space in the Court of the Gentiles as long as they gave Annas a portion of their profits. Merchants could make money exchanges and sell sheep, lambs, doves, pigeons, oil, wine, salt, and other requisites that go along with temple sacrifices.

Pilgrims paid dearly for these products and services. According to Jewish historian Alfred Edersheim, the price of a lamb could be ten times its value. Every offering was required to have the priests' approval, and the odds were that approval would be denied to offerings obtained outside the temple concessions. If a pilgrim from a small village raised a lamb and brought it to the temple as a sacrifice, most priests would say that lamb was unacceptable because it had not been purchased in the Court of the Gentiles.

The entire temple system—a system of extortion and robbery—was rigged to enrich temple priests. Those too poor to purchase lambs were allowed to buy pigeons and doves instead, according to the Levitical law. But merchants had a corner on that market as well. Priests would not approve birds brought in from the outside, and so even the poorest of the poor would pay ten or twenty times the actual value of the sacrifice. Foreigners who needed to exchange money were charged a twenty percent fee for the transaction.

When Jesus walked into the temple courtyard that day, he was met with the sights, sounds, and stench of a stockyard and the wrangling, haggling, and shouting of people bargaining over the price of animals. He understood completely the scene: He was looking at greed. He was looking at blasphemy. He was looking at robbery. The noise and the mess of crying, slaughtered animals, the blood flowing out the back of the temple created a chaotic scene. This was not worship. This was not reverence. This was not a house of prayer.

Jesus could have walked away. He could have let it go. After all, he had already cleaned house once before three years earlier and what good had it done? Why not ignore it? He was going to the cross anyway to bring salvation to the world and usher in a new age of God's redemptive work through a new covenant. The temple's days were numbered. What was the point of making a fuss?

But through his actions that day, I believe Jesus was telling his followers then and now that we must take a stand against injustice, hypocrisy, and greed. Eighteenth-century philosopher Edmond Burke famously wrote:

All that is needed for evil to triumph is for good men to do nothing.

The statement is as true today as it was 200 years ago. The way of the cross requires not only acknowledgement of unrighteousness; but we must also have the WILL to take a stand in the face of impossible opposition to refuse to allow evil to triumph.

Day 9: Authority

It is written, "My house will be called a house of prayer, but you are making it a den of robbers" (Matthew 21:13).

Then Jesus came to them and said, "All authority in heaven and on earth has been given to me" (Matthew 28:18).

In quoting Jeremiah 7:11, Jesus' message and divine authority were clear: "This is my house!" From the beginning, he announced his intention to carry out his father's work. While just a boy, Jesus told Mary and Joseph that he had to "be about his father's business" (Luke 2:49). If the house belongs to you, then you have the authority to clean it.

Interestingly, Jesus had cleared the temple once before, at the beginning of his public ministry (John 2). Thus, he started and completed his public ministry with a temple cleansing—two events that serve as bookends to his public life. I think there is a hidden meaning in that.

Jesus came to usher in a new kingdom, but it was not the kind of kingdom most people expected. Most people were looking for a messiah to challenge the power of Rome. But Jesus did not raise an army and go to Rome. Instead, he went to the temple in Jerusalem. Why? Because the kingdom he would establish was a spiritual kingdom concerned with humanity's relationship with God.

Jesus was not focused on politics or military power, but on worship, and the temple was the center of worship that represented a reconciled relationship between God and humanity. Jesus' message centered on true worship and the issues that flowed out of it, like morality and justice and religious truth.

That was who Jesus was and what he stood for and believed in. He was God incarnate with a mission to accomplish his father's business. At his ascension, Jesus reminded the apostles, "All authority has been given to me." Surely, everyone in the temple courtyard that day could sense Jesus' authority, and they bowed to it even though they could not have fully understood it.

Modern people recoil at the idea of moral authority. "You're not the boss of me" could be the motto of our age. People in our culture have a strong sense of personal liberty and moral independence. Moderns have bought into the idea that all truth is relative, and if it feels good and it doesn't hurt other people, then go for it! But there is an inherent problem in not believing in moral absolutes.

I read recently about leaders of a large British bank who gathered in their London boardroom with their executives to talk about the aftermath of the 2008 banking crisis. These bankers from around the world discussed implementing internal rules to insure their institution would move forward with new standards of morality and ethics. Like most global financial institutions at the time, this bank had been rocked to the core by the unethical practices that led to the Great Recession. But the discussion about moral practices never got off the ground because one of the executives asked a simple question that no one could answer:

"Whose morals?"

The problem with moral relativism is that it falls in on itself: To believe "there is no such thing as absolute truth" is to believe that statement is absolutely true, thus contradicting the premise! In his book, *The Abolition of Man*, C. S. Lewis wrote:

> *You can't go on "seeing through" things*

forever. The whole point of seeing through something is to see something through it. To "see through" all things is the same as not to see.

People don't believe they need moral authority until they really need it. The truth is that none of us wants to live in a universe where there are no rules and no sense of justice. Even the most hardened atheist believes murder, rape, and genocide are evil and wrong. People who resist the idea of a just and holy God still have to admit that the world needs some kind of moral compass when it comes to issues such as racial injustice or the exploitation of the poor. So where do we get that kind of moral authority?

I have to believe that question was on people's minds when Jesus turned over the tables. Part of the reason the crowds passively allowed him to continue his rampage through the market may have been because in the back of their minds, they believed his anger was absolutely justified.

The courtyard of the temple with all of its greed, robbery, and religious hypocrisy was a pretty good reflection of the human condition. A good cleansing was needed by someone with the moral authority to do it. The same is needed in every human heart, and that's where Jesus comes in. D. A. Carson observed in *A Call to Spiritual Transformation:*

> *If God had perceived that our greatest need was economic, he would have sent an economist. If he had perceived that our greatest need was entertainment, he would have sent us a comedian or an artist. If God had perceived that our greatest need was political stability, he would have sent us a politician. If he had perceived that our greatest need was health, he would have sent us a doctor. But he perceived that our greatest need involved our sin, our alienation from him, our profound rebellion, our death; and he sent us a Savior.*

Day 10: Power

When Jesus had finished these words, the crowds were amazed at His teaching; for He was teaching them as one having authority, and not as their scribes (Matthew 7:28–29).

For by Him all things were created, both in the heavens and on earth, visible and invisible, whether thrones or dominions or rulers or authorities—all things have been created through Him and for Him (Colossians 1:16).

If Jesus can cleanse a temple, he can cleanse a life. In more than thirty years as a pastor, I've seen it over and again. I've seen alcoholics who had lost everything be fully restored to their families. I've seen hopeless meth addicts be transformed to lead recovery ministries. I've seen a former madam of a house of prostitution come to Christ and work tirelessly to rescue young women from sex slavery in San Pedro Sula, Honduras. I've seen Muslim men and women come to Christ through dreams and become bold witnesses to other Muslims for the Gospel of Christ. I've watched a Buddhist woman come to Christ in Sri Lanka after the devastating tsunami and offer her home as the first house church in her village. I've seen the hopeless restored to hope, rebellious children return to their families, and absent dads come home to lead their families as godly men.

Brennan Manning tells the story of a former alcoholic who came to Christ and changed his ways. He was ridiculed by some of his drinking buddies for believing in Jesus.

"Do you really believe Jesus turned water into wine?" one of them asked one day.

"I don't know how Jesus turned water into wine," he said, "but I do know that for me, Jesus did something much more practical. He turned beer into furniture!"

I have seen the power of Jesus up close and personal, and I know that power is real.

The most powerful place in Judea was the temple. The high priest was a powerful man, and the one next to him was equally powerful. The head of the temple police was powerful, and all the myriad orders of priests wielded power, too.

Their temple's entire organizational structure also was very strong with great authority within the temple precinct area. For instance, the Romans had given temple authorities the right to kill Gentiles who simply walked past the Gate Beautiful.

But when Jesus appeared on the scene, the temple authorities met someone over whom they had absolutely no power. If you think Jesus was some meek and lowly person, you ought to study this event a little more deeply. There is no power like the power of Jesus!

Who knows how many thousands of people were in the temple courts that day, but we can have a pretty good idea that those kinds of merchants, extortionists, money-grabbing, money-hungry people wanted to cling to their wealth. They were not likely to relinquish their prosperity easily. Business people want to stay in business, and temple priests do not like being shamed on their own turf.

Religious leaders would not have accepted a would-be Galilean messiah exposing them in front of the swelling crowds of Passover pilgrims. It seems incredibly unlikely that one man could have thrown them all out, but that is exactly what happened. By sheer force of his personality, he cleared the courtyard. They could not stop him.

How did Jesus do it?

The Bible doesn't say, but it does say that Jesus threw them out. Maybe just his word was enough: "OUT!" With a word Jesus raised Lazarus, and with a word he spoke creation into existence. He could have done it with a word, but the text indicates that Jesus used both word and action. In other accounts of the event, Jesus physically turned over tables, demonstrating not only his vocal authority, but his physical presence as well.

In other words, despite their power, strength, and religious fortitude, the forces against him that day were no match for the power of Jesus. There is no power like the power of Jesus. There is no stronghold he cannot pull down or table he cannot turn. There is no demon he cannot banish. No chain he cannot break. No mountain he cannot move. No storm he cannot calm or crowd he cannot feed. There is no life too desperate, no addiction too overwhelming, no prodigal too far away, no problem too big for his power.

The same power that cleared the temple can cleanse your life. The same power that raised Jesus from the grave lives in us:

The Spirit of God, who raised Jesus from the dead, lives in you. And just as God raised

Christ Jesus from the dead, he will give life to your mortal bodies by this same Spirit living within you (Romans 8:11).

Day 11: Temple

Now set your heart and your soul to seek the LORD your God; arise, therefore, and build the sanctuary of the LORD God, so that you may bring the ark of the covenant of the LORD and the holy vessels of God into the house that is to be built for the name of the LORD (1 Chronicles 22:19).

To some people, the temple seems like an irrelevant concept, a mysterious religious relic for primitive people. "What does the temple have to do with modern people?" you may ask.

Let me explain why the temple has incredible significance and meaning to biblical faith. To understand the temple is first to understand the Garden of Eden. The garden was where God dwelt in perfect relationship with his creation, where there was life and complete fulfillment. The garden was a place of shalom, of human flourishing and of perfect love, joy, and bliss. Because the presence of God was there, no imperfection, no death, decay, or deformity could exist.

But when Adam and Eve rebelled against God, chose to make their own way, and to seek other means for their fulfillment, they were removed from the garden. The cost of their revolt against God was the loss of shalom (which means perfect peace and abundant flourishing in every way). They were forced from the sanctuary.

Now here the biblical account gets very strange. When Adam and Eve left the garden, God put a flaming sword to guard the entrance:

> *After he drove the man out, he placed on the east side of the Garden of Eden cherubim and a flaming sword flashing back and forth to guard the way to the tree of life* (Genesis 3:24).

This symbolism is very significant for our understanding of redemption and the meaning of the temple. The only way back into the presence of God is to come under the sword. There had to be sacrifice. God's instructions to Solomon for the design of the temple included immaculate detail for the Holy of Holies, which was intended to symbolize the beauty of the garden and a way back into

God's sanctuary.

But who can survive the sword? Who can survive the justice of God? That is the question of the ages that the temple partially answers. At the center of the temple was the Holy of Holies, basically a cube with a thick veil on one side that concealed the Shekinah, or glory of God. The Holy of Holies was a physical representation of the sanctuary that Adam and Eve enjoyed in the garden. Outside the garden, however, the glory of God was a fearful, dangerous thing. People did not survive the presence of God. Only the high priest could gain entry into the Holy of Holies, and then only after immaculate plans and personal sacrifices. Thus, the Holy of Holies served as a reminder that humanity could not work its way back into a perfect relationship with God. Sacrifice offered a way in, but that way was incomplete, a mere shadow of things to come.

Why would God require sacrifice? I believe we know instinctively that sacrifice is important to reconciliation. If you have experienced some kind of abuse in your life, or have been wronged in some significant way, you know it is not enough for an abuser simply to say "Sorry!" and expect to move on as if nothing had happened. You know in your heart that there has to be some kind of price paid in order for justice to be done—not vindictiveness or revenge, but justice.

God dwells in perfect justice, and therefore, cosmic rebellion and sin against God requires cosmic payment. That is what the flaming sword is—cosmic justice.

The temple reminded people that in order to get back into relationship with God, a blood sacrifice must be made. The temple also pointed to a better day of restoration and fulfillment through the coming messiah. The Old Testament prophets told of a day when the glory of the Lord would cover the earth.

> *Every pot in Jerusalem and Judah will be holy to the LORD Almighty, and all who come to sacrifice will take some of the pots and cook in them* (Zechariah 14:21).

The pots in the Holy of Holies could only be used by the high priest, but Zechariah said that when the messiah comes, every pot in Jerusalem will be as holy as those pots. In other words, the very presence of the messiah would replace the need for the temple. God would mercifully restore our relationship to him by some other way. Isaiah said this about the coming of the messiah:

> *You will go out in joy and be led forth in peace; the mountains and hills will burst into song before you, and all the trees of the field will clap their hands* (Isaiah 55:12).

The Old Testament prophecies include great anticipation for the coming of the messiah and how his redemptive work would restore all of God's creation. When Jesus entered the temple, he served notice that he was the expected messiah, and new arrangements were ready to be made!

Think about what happened at the cross: Jesus took the blow from the fiery sword and offered his body and his blood as the final sin offering for all people for all eternity!

> *For by one offering he has perfected forever those being sanctified* (Hebrews 10:14).

> *Christ himself is the propitiation for our sins, and not for ours only but for the whole world* (1 John 2:1–2).

When Jesus died on the cross, the veil in the temple was ripped through, a dramatic demonstration that the Holy of Holies and the entire sacrificial system with all its clean laws was no longer needed. Jesus is the ultimate sacrifice for sin, and now Jesus makes us clean. He is the promised Messiah foreshadowed by the temple.

The book of Hebrews explains that Christ did not so much abolish the Old Testament ceremonial laws as fulfilled them. Therefore, whenever we pray in Jesus' name, we "have confidence to enter the Most Holy Place by the blood of Jesus" (Hebrews 10:19).

> *Jesus is our way in.*
> *He is the lamb without blemish.*
> *He is the promised Messiah.*
> *He is the Bread of Life.*
> *He is the fulfillment of the temple!*

Sunday Reflection: Entry to Jerusalem

Read Mark 11:1–33.

1. Why did Jesus ride into Jerusalem on a donkey and not a war horse?

2. What does this say about the humility of Jesus?

3. What does it say about our need for humility?

4. What did Jesus do once he arrived in Jerusalem?

5. What is the meaning of the temple?

6. How does Jesus replace the need for the temple?

Week Two: Entry to Jerusalem

Week Three: Betrayal of Judas

John 13:17–30

Day 12: Betrayal

After he had said this, Jesus was troubled in spirit and testified, "Very truly I tell you, one of you is going to betray me" (John 13:21).

I'm an Oklahoma City Thunder fan, so I know a thing or two about betrayal. For nine years, I invested enthusiastically in season tickets so my son and I could go to basketball games and scream and yell for the blue and orange. We've faithfully cheered our way through six playoff seasons and have the T-shirts to prove it. We've put a lot of blood, sweat, and tears into our team. Okay, maybe not blood, but at least sweat and tears.

Then this year the unthinkable happened: The face of our franchise, the one guy we could always depend on to be there with a last second jump shot or merciless dunk on the opposing team, the one guy we could never replace, Kevin "Judas" Durant, decided he'd rather play for the disgusting Golden State Warriors.

Maybe I'm being dramatic. But I just finished watching the first game between my Thunder and the hated Warriors since the infamous betrayal, and it was not pretty. Judas Durant scored about a thousand points, and our team went down in flames. And worse, he seemed to enjoy it.

Yes, I know a thing or two about betrayal, and chances are you do, too. Perhaps the betrayal you have experienced is on a much bigger scale than that of a spurned sports fan. Maybe you've been betrayed by a spouse, co-workers, a parent, or your own children. Maybe a good friend stabbed you in the back or someone you depended on to hold your heart carelessly broke your trust.

One thing is for sure, betrayal is a part of life. Because we live in a fallen world with fallen people, someone inevitably will let us down. And when they do, we often compare them to Judas. Judas takes the cake on betrayal. It is difficult to comprehend how a man can spend twenty-four hours a day for three years with the Lord Jesus, and then sell him out for a few pieces of silver.

Today's text says that Jesus was troubled in his spirit by the betrayal. Clearly, he was hurt by it, as we can feel the sting in his statement to Judas: *"You betray me with a kiss?"* (Luke 22:48)

Even the Son of Man felt the pain of betrayal.

What stings most about betrayal is the feeling that we are not valued. For instance, when a woman learns her husband is leaving her for another woman, she may slowly realize that her husband and the other woman have secretly been planning the separation for a long time. The earth-shattering decision she is about to endure was made without her having a chance to be involved. The betrayal hurts because she was not valued, and additionally, she was not given the dignity of knowing what was going on behind her back.

That sense of not being valued is at the heart of the hurt of betrayal. If you have been betrayed, I want you to consider what Jesus endured on his way to the cross. One of his closest friends betrayed him and devalued him to the degree that he was willing to trade his friendship for a few lousy coins. There are several really important lessons for all of us here.

First, being betrayed does not mean you are a bad person. The story of Judas' betrayal of Jesus reminds us that even the Lord Jesus was betrayed by a close friend. If Jesus can be betrayed, anyone can be betrayed. Being betrayed is not a reflection on your character; it is a reflection on the character of the one doing the betraying.

Second, the story of Judas is a reminder that there is nothing that happens in this life that Jesus cannot understand. When you feel betrayed and devalued by someone close to you, you can allow the Spirit of Christ to wash over you with the knowledge that he understands on a deeply divine level what it means to be betrayed. Let him comfort you in your grief with the knowledge that he identifies with your hurt. If you've been betrayed, remember that you are in good company!

Third and most important, when you feel devalued because of an act of betrayal, remember the truth of the Gospel: The God of the universe loves us so much, he was willing to die for us. The love of God is so vast that he loves everyone in the world as if each person were the only one to love. When you understand the Gospel on that deep level, you know you are loved and valued by God. You may not be able to change the circumstances around your betrayal, but you CAN redefine and recalibrate the way you feel about those circumstances.

Jesus took our betrayal onto himself so that we would never have to feel betrayed. It is the reality that changes the picture for us. That is the power of the Gospel working in our hearts.

Day 13: Bitterness

So Jesus told him, "What you are about to do, do quickly." But no one at the meal understood why Jesus said this to him. Since Judas had charge of the money, some thought Jesus was telling him to buy what was needed for the festival, or to give something to the poor. As soon as Judas had taken the bread, he went out. And it was night. When he was gone, Jesus said, "Now the Son of Man is glorified and God is glorified in him. If God is glorified in him, God will glorify the Son in himself, and will glorify him at once. My children, I will be with you only a little longer. You will look for me, and just as I told the Jews, so I tell you now: Where I am going, you cannot come. A new command I give you: Love one another. As I have loved you, so you must love one another. By this everyone will know that you are my disciples, if you love one another" (John 13:27–34).

It took a while for the disciples to realize that Judas had betrayed Jesus. Apparently, they never saw it coming, so complete was Judas' deception.

Interestingly, in John's account of the confrontation with Judas, Jesus immediately pivoted to a lesson about glorifying God and loving one another. He did not dwell on the betrayal or sulk about it; instead, he focused on how to glorify God.

We can draw a great lesson about overcoming bitterness from this encounter. When we have been hurt, we naturally feel angry, hurt, or even depressed. How can we deal with these emotions responsibly and appropriately? The Bible gives clear instruction on what to do with anger:

> *See to it that no one falls short of the grace of God and that no bitter root grows up to cause trouble and defile man* (Hebrews 12:15).

If we hold on to resentment, then we allow others to control us. When you say, "That person makes me so mad!" you are admitting that you are under that person's control. The only way to overcome bitterness is to focus on the grace of God.

Have you ever known a family that was poisoned by one

person's attitude? Bitterness is contagious and can manifest into a family pattern that lasts years, even generations. Remember the rule that we tend to become like the people we hang out with the most. Someone must have the spiritual and emotional fortitude to break the chain.

And there's only one way to do that—through grace.

In truth, without grace in our lives, we will become bitter. Why? Because we live in a broken world and fallen people hurt one another. Hurt people hurt people. People who are feeling hurt will inevitably hurt others. Inevitably, you will have many reasons to feel betrayed and hurt in the course of your life. So the ability to receive and extend grace is one of the most important qualities we can ever learn.

> *In your anger do not sin; do not let the sun go down on your anger* (Ephesians 4:26).

Notice the Bible does not say that anger is sin, but only what we do with our anger. Anger is a perfectly natural, God-given emotion that serves as a flashing red light to warn us that something needs to change. How we use our anger can either be life-giving or life-taking.

When we feel anger, we have three ways to respond: We can EXPRESS it, but that only hurts others; we can SUPPRESS it, but that only hurts us; or we can CONFESS it, which is the healthy, proactive response. Let's look at all three of these responses as we think about how to overcome bitterness.

Expressing anger by lashing out with hurtful words is a natural response, but one that only spews bitterness and is never productive. In fact, using words to hurt others or to try to even the score only makes the situation worse. Bitterness is the poison we drink to hurt others. If we use angry words to get revenge, we only hurt ourselves. Expressing anger as a way to get back at others is destructive and sinful.

> *Do not let any unwholesome talk come out of your mouths, but only what is helpful for building others up according to their needs, that it may benefit those who listen* (Ephesians 4:29 NIV).

Your mother was right when she told you, "If you can't say something nice, don't say anything at all." The Bible teaches us that our words should be wholesome and helpful. That doesn't mean that we can't speak the truth in love or say hard things when they need to be said, but our words should be measured and productive with the aim to build others up and not tear them down.

Suppressing our anger can be just as unhealthy as expressing it. Many people respond to anger by becoming withdrawn and sullen, pushing their anger down into the pit of their stomachs. But anger doesn't reside calmly and peacefully within our spirits; rather, it joins with other unhealthy emotions and plans an insurrection. "Do not let the sun go down on your anger," the Bible teaches. In other words, don't ignore it or suppress it, but deal with it positively. That is the most helpful and productive response to anger.

The Bible teaches that the proper response to anger is to confess it. In other words, we should talk to God about our feelings to get the proper perspective on them. Anger is not a first emotion—it does not simply drop out of the sky from nowhere. Rather, anger is a second or third emotion that comes from something. We need to know the source so we can deal with it properly.

Some people advise counting to 100 when we get angry, but I have found that response doesn't help: I only became better at counting! What is helpful is to pray and confess. Maybe you need to confess that you are not good at forgiving, or that you have made an idol of self, and now that your idol is threatened, you feel angry. Maybe you need to confess that you have bitter feelings toward someone, and you can't get them out of your mind. When we confess our anger, we can trace it

82

to its source and turn it over to God.

The only way to overcome bitterness is to confess it and forgive.

One day Peter asked Jesus how many times we should forgive others, suggesting that maybe seven times would be appropriate. But Jesus answered, *"I tell you, not seven times, but seven times seventy"* (Matthew 18:23). Jesus didn't mean that we should forgive 490 times and then we could stop! He used exaggeration to say that every time we feel hurt or bitterness in our hearts, we should forgive.

"But that person does not deserve to be forgiven," you might say. You are absolutely right; however, forgiveness is not about fairness, but righteousness. It's about grace. We don't forgive a person because it's the FAIR thing to do. We forgive a person because it's the RIGHT thing to do, and we don't want hearts full of poison. We don't want our hearts holding on to hurt and hate.

Forgiveness is free, but it is not cheap. It cost Jesus his life. It cost God his son. And as Jesus was dying on the cross, with his arms outstretched and the blood dripping down, he said, "Father, forgive them! They don't know what they're doing," or in other words, "Father, I know they don't deserve it, but I love them, so forgive them."

And if forgiveness is good enough for Jesus, it's good enough for us.

Day 14: Religiousness

Just as he was speaking, Judas, one of the Twelve, appeared. With him was a crowd armed with swords and clubs, sent from the chief priests, the teachers of the law, and the elders. Now the betrayer had arranged a signal with them: "The one I kiss is the man; arrest him and lead him away under guard." Going at once to Jesus, Judas said, "Rabbi!" and kissed him. The men seized Jesus and arrested him (Mark 14:43-46).

There are few things I hate worse in this life than religion. I know that sounds crazy coming from a pastor, but let me explain. Religion is the attempt to reach God by our own merits. Religion is man-made and often exploitive and manipulative. Every religion in the world except Christianity says something like, "If you work really hard at these requirements you can cross over the bridge to ultimate fulfillment." Religion is humanity reaching up to God, but Christianity is God reaching down to humanity. There is a BIG difference.

The difference is that one is human-centered, and the other is God-centered. One has everything to do with what humans can accomplish, and the other has everything to do with what God has already accomplished. One says, "I must do these things so that God will love me," while the other says, "God loves me so I will do these things." Do you see the difference?

New York City pastor and theologian, Tim Keller, was asked to speak at a conference with the theme, "Why Religion is the Biggest Problem in the World." Obviously, the organizers wanted Keller to be their token Christian speaker at the event, and the topic felt somewhat insulting. But Keller decided to accept. "I realized I agreed with them," he said. "Religion IS a big problem in the world—that's why we need Jesus!"

I completely agree. Christianity is not about religion— it is about a relationship. Unlike any religion, Christianity teaches that salvation comes by grace through faith, not by works (Ephesians 2:8).

Someone will say, "But I hear Christians talking about living sexually pure lives and keeping their temple clean and loving other people more than themselves—all of those things seem like religious works. Of course, Christianity is a religion because it calls people to live a certain way." To a certain extent, that view is true, but these behavioral changes come about as a result of the redemption Jesus accomplished on the cross and from the Holy Spirit's presence in our hearts. That relationship changes us, not religious works.

First-century Israel was enslaved by religious works. The Jewish ruling council, the Sanhedrin, was in essence the supreme court of Israel. Some of its members belonged to the sect of the Sadducees, who were religious liberals; others to the Pharisees, who were religious conservatives. Within the Pharisees was a group of scribes who were the law experts. But they all were religious leaders so caught up in their religiousness, their status and power, that they were anesthetized to biblical faith.

The sects within the Sanhedrin rarely agreed on anything, much less how to interpret Scripture. For instance, the Sadducees didn't believe in the resurrection, an afterlife, or angels, but the Pharisees believed in all of that. Their disagreements were deep, but they did agree about Jesus: They hated him and wanted him dead (with the exception of Joseph of Arimathea and Nicodemus).

They were jealous of his power, for who of them could raise the dead? Give sight to the blind? Hearing to the deaf? A voice to the mute? Who could make people walk? Heal them of all diseases? Deliver them from demons? Who could create food? Control storms?

They also envied Jesus' popularity. They hated his message of repentance of sin and the gift of salvation by grace. They taught that salvation was awarded for strict religious behavior and compliance to moral law. They were proud and self-righteous and wanted to earn their salvation. That is what religion does to you.

The religious leaders hated Jesus because his popularity encroached on their space. As Jesus asserted his authority, they felt powerless against it. When they heard that he had raised a man from the dead in Bethany, they were frightened by his popularity and credibility. They were even more frightened by his triumphal entry into Jerusalem on his ridiculous donkey as thousands of people laid palm branches in front of him. Their hatred grew the next day when he single-handedly cleared the marketplace where the Sanhedrin ran temple operations like an Israeli mafia, taking their percentage from the greedy merchants. "A den of robbers!" Jesus called it. They cowered at the sound of his voice and the strength of his character as he drove them all out.

Those three days sealed Jesus' fate. He had to be stopped, and they knew they had to be the ones to do it. They wanted him dead, but they dared not arrest him publicly because they would incite a riot (Mark 14:1). They needed to strike when Jesus was away from the crowds, but that required an insider, a spy among his disciples. That person came willingly, and his name was Judas.

> *Then Judas Iscariot, one of the Twelve, went to the chief priests to betray Jesus to them* (Mark 14:10).

The rest is history. The betrayal of Jesus led to his arrest and his arrest to crucifixion. Although Jesus knew what he was doing and was in total control of his own fate, the outcome of his final days was brought about by betrayal and because of what works-based religion does to the human heart.

Religious people tend to take pride in their moral behavior and to look down on others who don't meet their standards. If their tightly held belief system is threatened, they respond in anger and condemnation because their very self-worth is at risk. Religion is bondage because it enslaves people to works and moralism. Religion also makes people vulnerable to insecurity and feelings of inadequacy when they are not living up to their own standards.

Religious people tend to swing between two poles of feeling proud and superior to others on one hand and feeling worthless and inadequate on the other. Religion is a trap, the very opposite of the Gospel. The Gospel builds up, but religion puffs up. The Gospel sets us free, but religion places us in bondage. The Gospel brings life, but religion brings death. The Gospel restores, but religion destroys. The Gospel opens eyes, but religion closes minds.

Religious leaders could not see the true Messiah standing in front of them and sent Jesus to the cross. That is what religion does: It blinds us to the truth and hardens our hearts to the true Gospel. That is why there are few things in this life that I hate more than religion.

Day 15: Scripture

I am not referring to all of you; I know those I have chosen. But this is to fulfill this passage of Scripture: "He who shared my bread has turned against me." I am telling you now before it happens, so that when it does happen you will believe that I am who I am. Very truly I tell you, whoever accepts anyone I send accepts me; and whoever accepts me accepts the one who sent me (John 13:18–20).

I think most people believe that Jesus walked around the earth with a godlike knowledge of everything happening around him at all times. We tend to look at the stories of his life with the idea that Jesus must have floated on air above everyone else, had foreknowledge of people's thoughts and actions, and could leap tall buildings with a single bound. Maybe we see him as a sort of Marvel comics superhero, only with divine powers.

But in Philippians we read that Jesus "made himself nothing and took the very nature of a man and was made in human likeness" (Philippians 2:17). In other words, Jesus set aside his own glory and his divine nature while on earth to take on human flesh and become like us in every way. Although he was God, Jesus limited himself to the very same resources in this life that you and I have to work with in ours. There was nothing that Jesus utilized in his life that you and I cannot access in ours. Paul, the apostle, made this observation to the Roman, Cornelius:

> *God anointed Jesus of Nazareth with the Holy Spirit and power, and how he went around doing good and healing all who were under the power of the devil, because God was with him* (Acts 10:38).

Jesus was guided by the power of the Holy Spirit, the same power available to us as well. He had God's presence, and you and I have that, too. He had the Scriptures to guide him just as we have. We are afforded the very same things in this life that Jesus had during his lifetime. Jesus was able to live a perfect life without blemish because of the assurances of God, the Spirit of God, and the word of God.

In John 13, Jesus explained to the disciples that their

lives were about to get very dark. He would be betrayed, arrested, and taken to the cross, and their lives would be rocked like they could not imagine. But then he said to them:

> *"But this is to fulfill this passage of scripture..."*

Here is an important truth I don't want us to miss on our journey toward the cross. Jesus told the disciples they could endure their struggle by understanding the meaning of the Bible's teachings. He said to them, in effect, "When life gets hard over the next few days as I'm betrayed and taken to the cross, you should have it in your heart that all of these things are happening because Scripture said they would happen."

He taught the disciples to know, believe, and trust the word of God. By meditating on the word of God and knowing and believing its teaching, Jesus was able to pass through suffering, and he wanted his disciples to have the very same understanding, the same resources. He wants that for us as well. "Believe the Bible," he said to them. "Learn it and be saturated by its teaching and you will get through any struggle because of its promises."

Over and again in the Gospels, Jesus said his life was the fulfilment of the Scriptures. In all his teachings, he referred to the divine authority of the Old Testament (Matthew 5:17–18, 8:17, 12:40–42; Luke 4:18–21, 10:25–28, 15:29–31, 17:32, 24:25–45; John 5:39–47). He quoted the Old Testament seventy-eight times, the Pentateuch alone twenty-six times. He quoted from Genesis, Exodus, Leviticus, Deuteronomy, Psalms, Proverbs, Isaiah, Jeremiah, Ezekiel, Daniel, Hosea, Amos, Jonah, Micah, and Malachi. He referred to the Old Testament as "the Scriptures," "the word of God," and "the wisdom of God." Jesus was very careful to align to biblical teachings. In the Sermon on the Mount, Jesus said:

> *For truly I tell you, until heaven and earth disappear, not the smallest letter, not the least stroke of a pen, will by any means disappear from the Law until everything is accomplished* (Matthew 5:17).

Jesus believed that every word of the Bible was true, the word of God, and that it would be fulfilled in him. If we are to access all the resources we need to get through life's inevitable struggles, we must believe it, too. We must believe in God's promises and recognize that our lives fit into the bigger story of God's redemptive work, as taught in Scripture. That is what Jesus did his entire life on earth.

During the unspeakable trials of his final week, Jesus was able to focus his heart on the bigger perspective of God's eternal plan and to find assurance in God's presence and guidance from his word. Those same resources are available to you and me today.

Day 16: Disillusionment

Then when Judas, his betrayer, saw that Jesus was condemned, he changed his mind and brought back the thirty pieces of silver to the chief priests and the elders, saying, "I have sinned by betraying innocent blood." They said, "What is that to us? See to it yourself." And throwing down the pieces of silver into the temple, he departed, and he went and hanged himself (Matthew 27:3-5).

The story of Judas may be the greatest tragedy in human history. His very name through the ages will be associated with traitorous betrayal. Judas is a tragic example of what it means to have opportunity and then lose it. He is an example of the tragedy of disillusionment, his story made more terrible in light of his promising beginning.

Judas followed the same Jesus as the other disciples. For three years, day in and day out, he heard the same teaching, saw the same miracles, and participated in the same ministries. He had all the same experiences and resources as all other followers, and yet he did not become what the others became. He became the opposite. Their belief grew, and his faltered. They became more confident, he more doubtful. They became more joyful, he more disillusioned. While the other disciples were becoming servants of Christ and apostles who would lead thousands, Judas became a spiteful, small, bitter lump of clay in the hands of Satan.

From the beginning, Judas wanted something different from the others. He did not take on discipleship to serve the purposes of Christ, but to serve his own. He was not a part of the fellowship because of what he could offer others, but to seek his own agenda, looking for the advantages Jesus could bring him. Judas did not seek God's glory; he wanted his own.

Jesus knew Judas' heart:

> *"You are clean, but not all of you." For He knew the one who was betraying him* (Mark 10–11).

Judas sat and listened all through Jesus' lesson on humility and the washing of the disciples' feet. Jesus even washed Judas' feet. Judas sat there, pretending to be a loyal follower, knowing that the die had already been cast on his betrayal. He allowed the Savior to clean his dirty feet and dry them with a towel knowing he was plotting his arrest.

Jesus knew Judas would betray him, and yet Jesus reached out to him, washing his feet anyway. The measures Jesus took to win Judas even at this late hour make his love even more astounding. The experience of having Jesus wash his feet should be enough to break any man's heart. But not Judas. He sat there cold-hearted, determined to sell Jesus out to the executioners.

How did he get there? How does a man walk with the Savior for three years, day and night, and yet become hard and disillusioned? I believe all disillusionment begins at the altar of self. The core issue in our sinful condition is our tendency to put self at the center of all things. Charles Swindoll once described this self-centeredness as "ingrown eyeballs," the belief that all of life is about oneself. That is what blinded Judas to the glory of Christ. While others saw miracles, Judas asked, "What's in it for me?"

Disillusionment happens when we focus more on the "kingdom of me" than the Kingdom of God.

Many people get into Christianity thinking it's all about them, building them up, making them happy, wealthy, and wise. They misinterpret Jesus' teaching on the "abundant life" (John 10:10) to mean they will have perfect health, a comfortable lifestyle, full realization of their dreams, and instant relief from their problems through faith and prayer. They expect the Christian life to be easy—heaven on earth.

But heaven doesn't exist on earth; rather, earth is preparation for heaven. In this life, God is equipping us with the kinds of eternal qualities we will need in heaven. God is more interested in our character than our comfort because he has an eternal perspective. God is not your genie, and life is not supposed to be easy. When good things happen that's called a blessing, but when bad things happen that's just called life. In fact, God uses hardship to make us better "heaven people."

The lesson of Judas is that when we insist that life is all about us, our hopes and dreams, we will never see the miracle and glory of God's work all around us. We were not created to be gods, but we were created to be godly. God is not our servant, and if we fall for the idea that life is about us, we will follow the path of Judas, and that is the way of disillusionment and self-destruction.

Day 17: Reconciliation

Jesus answered, "I tell you, Peter, before the rooster crows today, you will deny three times that you know me" (Luke 22:34).

Meanwhile, Simon Peter was still standing there warming himself. So they asked him, "You aren't one of his disciples too, are you?" He denied it, saying, "I am not." One of the high priest's servants, a relative of the man whose ear Peter had cut off, challenged him, "Didn't I see you with him in the garden?" Again Peter denied it, and at that moment a rooster began to crow (John 18:25–27).

The third time he said to him, "Simon, son of John, do you love me?" Peter was hurt because Jesus asked him the third time, "Do you love me?" He said, "Lord, you know all things; you know that I love you." Jesus said, "Feed my sheep" (John 21:17).

Simon Peter blew it. He denied his Lord, the one thing he promised he would never do. How easy it is to be strong away from the heat of the battle! How fragile we are when the vice is closing in! Proud, determined Peter had folded instead of standing for Christ. We've all been there. We've all done things to be ashamed of, things we believed we would never do. How can we be so weak, so stupid, and how can Jesus ever forgive us?

And yet Jesus not only forgave Peter, he challenged him to feed his sheep, to see himself as a leader in the church, and to look to the future. He restored Peter, reassuring him that he was loved, and Jesus will do the same for us if we come to him as Peter did.

On our journey to the cross this week, we have focused on one of the great tragedies in Scripture, the betrayal of Judas. That is a lot of time to spend on such a negative story. So let's finish the week on a positive note. Instead of examining the tragic results of turning our backs on the Savior, let's see what happens when we are reconciled to him. In other words, what if Judas had found his way back? What if Judas had taken the path of the Apostle Peter, who denied Jesus three times and then was reconciled to him after the resurrection? These two men's stories provide a stark contrast for how to approach failure.

There is an important lesson to explore here because many of us have had terrible failures in life, and we may wonder if we can recover. "How could God ever forgive me?" is a frequent question I hear as pastor.

I recently counseled a young woman who was racked by guilt over a tragic decision in her past. She clung to guilt, believing forgiveness was impossible. She dared not tell anyone about her experience, especially not people from church or family members who she believed would recoil in horror and never speak to her again. Her thoughts were irrational, of course, but they are emblematic of how the enemy works to accentuate the negative and cause us to believe the very worst about ourselves and others.

Her guilt had the same effect on her spirit as kryptonite has on Superman: It sapped her strength, joy, and life. She could not find peace in Scripture or at church or even in her marriage. Guilt had dragged her into a pit so deep she saw no hope of ever climbing out.

Like Peter, she needed the risen Savior to lift her out. She needed to know the grace and love that is deeper than any pit. As Corrie Ten Boom famously said in *The Hiding Place*:

*There is no pit so deep that God's love is
not deeper still!*

I will never forget the joy that came back in this young
woman's life when she took hold of God's grace and
forgiveness. She shared her story with family and others,
who cried with her and shared Jesus' love with her. She
is now determined to use her story to help others in a
similar situation to heal.

I never tire of watching others transformed by the
power of God's grace and forgiveness. Jesus said, "He
who is forgiven much, loves much" (Luke 7:47). I know
that is true. I have watched it happen over and again in
thirty years of ministry. People who have been radically
forgiven are people who show radical grace.

Radical forgiveness is what made Peter such an
effective leader. He had been through the fire and had
been refined by it. Jesus showed Peter mercy, and he was
forever changed because of it. He would later write of
that mercy in his first letter to the church:

> *Praise be to the God and Father of our Lord
> Jesus Christ! In his great mercy he has given
> us new birth into a living hope through the
> resurrection of Jesus Christ from the dead,
> and into an inheritance that can never*

perish, spoil or fade. This inheritance is kept in heaven for you, who through faith are shielded by God's power until the coming of the salvation that is ready to be revealed in the last time. In all this you greatly rejoice, though now for a little while you may have had to suffer grief in all kinds of trials. These have come so that the proven genuineness of your faith—of greater worth than gold, which perishes even though refined by fire—may result in praise, glory and honor when Jesus Christ is revealed (1 Peter 1:3–7).

Here is one of the wonderful mysteries of God's grace: He can take our tragic mistakes and use them for his glory. God never wastes a pain. Maybe your life has taken a bad turn, and you think you have veered off course so badly that it can never be brought back. Maybe you think you are on plan B, D, or F. But here's the wonderful mystery of God's providence: As a follower of Jesus, you are never on plan B! You are only on plan A. God will take your bad choices, no matter how tragic or devastating, put them into the refiner's fire, and turn them into pure gold.

The Bible tells us not to cling to our guilt:

Look straight ahead with honest confi-

dence; don't hang your head in shame (Proverbs 4:25 TEV).

Yes, all have sinned and fallen short of God's glorious ideal; yet now God declares us "not guilty" of offending him if we trust in Jesus Christ, who in his kindness freely takes away our sins (Romans 3:23–24 TLB).

Many people know intellectually about God's forgiveness, but emotionally, they seem unable to receive it. Sometimes the hardest thing for people to do is to forgive themselves. But that's what the enemy wants: He wants us to be so tortured by guilt that we are no use to God's kingdom. Accept God's forgiveness and bring it deeply into your heart, and then forgive yourself!

Maybe you have been following a pattern of asking God for forgiveness over and again for the same sins. Quit doing that. You only have to ask God once, and your transgression is forgiven and forgotten. You only have to confess a sin one time, and God forgives and forgets. But you may have to forgive yourself hundreds of times before you fully realize that God has mercifully forgiven you.

Someone once asked Eleanor Roosevelt how she

accomplished so much in life. She replied, "I never waste time with regrets."

That's a great way to live. Stop clinging to guilt, and get back in the game.

You're still on plan A.

Sunday Reflection:
Betrayal of Judas

Read John 13:17–30.

1. Why do you think Judas was capable of betraying Jesus?

2. What made Judas different from the other disciples?

3. What does the story of Judas teach us about how we get through our betrayals?

4. What is the danger of projecting our own agenda on our relationship with Christ?

5. What was the difference between the tragedy of Judas and the reconciliation of Peter?

6. What can we learn about our plans and God's plans in the story of Peter?

Week Four: The Passover Meal

John 12:1–11, Matthew 26:1–29, Mark 14:22–26

Day 18: Worship

Six days before the Passover, Jesus came to Bethany, where Lazarus lived, whom Jesus had raised from the dead. Here a dinner was given in Jesus' honor. Martha served, while Lazarus was among those reclining at the table with him. Then Mary took about a pint of pure nard, an expensive perfume; she poured it on Jesus' feet and wiped his feet with her hair. And the house was filled with the fragrance of the perfume. But one of his disciples, Judas Iscariot, who was later to betray him, objected, "Why wasn't this perfume sold and the money given to the poor? It was worth a year's wages." He did not say this because he cared about the poor but because he was a thief; as keeper of the money bag, he used to help himself to what was put into it. "Leave her alone," Jesus replied. "It was intended that she should save this perfume for the day of my burial. You will always have the poor among you, but you will not always have me." Meanwhile a large crowd of Jews found out that Jesus was there and came, not only because of him but also to see Lazarus, whom he had raised from the dead. So the chief priests made plans to kill Lazarus as well, for on account of him many of the Jews were going over to Jesus and believing in him (John 12:1–11).

Mary may have been the first person to realize what Jesus was about to do. The disciples knew that Jesus had come to Jerusalem at a very precarious time, and thus, was in great danger. They had listened to Jesus' teachings that pointed to his coming death, but apparently they had not comprehended their full meaning.

But Mary seemed to get it. She took expensive perfume normally reserved for burials and poured it out on Jesus' feet in an act of extravagant worship and as a foreshadowing of Jesus' death. Weeks earlier, Mary had sat at Jesus' feet listening intently to his words while Martha was busy in the kitchen (Luke 10:38–42). Now she grasped what no one else seemed to understand: Jesus had to die.

Did she know that Jesus' death would take away the sins of the world? Did she understand that Jesus was the

Lamb of God who would be placed on the altar to fulfill the covenant of Abraham? Did she know Jesus was the embodiment of the Passover, as his teachings and the prophecies had said? Did she understand that Jesus was the fulfillment of the law and the prophecies about the Messiah and would replace the need for the temple? We cannot know for sure, but we do know Mary paid attention to Jesus. Mary was like that girl you want to sit next to in class because she knows the answers before anyone else—she got it.

But not Judas. Judas' mind was on other things. He wasn't concerned about fulfillment of prophecy or sacrifice for sins. Judas was concerned about Judas. He claimed he cared about the poor, but his hypocrisy was thinly veiled. He cared only about money. Those who care only about themselves can never truly worship because worship involves gratitude, honesty, and sacrifice. We see all three in Mary's anointing of Jesus.

First, we see her gratitude. The reason for the dinner, the text says, was to honor Jesus. Martha and Mary were throwing a party in Jesus' honor because he had raised their brother from the dead. Their hearts were full of gratitude for all that Jesus had done for them. That is what worship looks like—a deep gratitude for all Christ has done, for giving his life for us and raising us from the dead. The deeper we understand that reality, the better our worship.

Second, worship requires our honesty. Jesus told the woman at the well that "the kind of worshiper the Father seeks worships him in Spirit and in truth" (John 4:23). Judas could not worship Christ as Mary did because he was living a lie. If we do not come clean for who we really are, we will never truly worship.

Third, worship is about sacrifice. Jesus taught the disciples, "Where your treasure is, there will your heart be also" (Matthew 6:21). When you love someone, you will go to extravagant expense to show that love. If someone tells you they love you, but they are unwilling to sacrifice for you, that is not true love.

"Pure nard" or "spikenard," which comes from the Greek word "nardos," was an expensive, uncommon perfume extracted from grasses that grew in faraway India. Juices squeezed from the grasses were dried into a hard, lard-like substance, from which perfume was made through a lengthy, costly process. The cost of transporting spikenard from India to Judea only added to the cost of this rare product.

Spikenard was too expensive for most people, who had to settle for one of the many cheap imitations. But the word used in John 12:3 tells us that Mary didn't bring

Jesus a cheap imitation; she brought him the real thing—an ointment so valuable that it was normally reserved only for nobility. The cost of one jar was equivalent to an annual salary in first-century Jerusalem. And she poured the entire jar onto his feet. What an eye-popping, incredibly extravagant gift!

Think of the amazing demonstration of love from Mary—an annual wage! All who were there must have been shocked by the gesture. Think of giving all you earn in a year in one moment of lavish affection. Think of what she could have done with all that money. But her brother, Lazarus, had been dead and now was alive, and the Savior was before her. No amount of money or display of gratitude could come close to the joy that filled Mary's heart.

A few days earlier, Jesus had told Martha that he was the resurrection and the life, and that truth had become a glorious reality to Mary. There is no measuring the value of Jesus. There is no quantifying his worth, no way to calculate the cost of love. And so she poured this elaborately expensive jar onto his dirty, smelly, human feet. Why?

Because the least of Jesus is worthy of the best of us.

Then she cleaned his feet with her hair. Why didn't

she use a towel or a cloth? Her act was as if to say, "The cleanest thing I have to offer you is my hair." I love John Piper's words in *The Pursuit of Holiness* as he describes Mary's act of devotion:

> *Jesus, cleanness and sweetness befit you and your purity and holiness and power and grace. But as for me, dirt and odors befit me. My hair is the most beautiful and the most clean thing I have. But if it could serve to magnify your purity and your sweetness, it would be my honor to turn it into a rag for your feet.*

What an unforgettable act of worship by a woman who saw the splendor of Christ's work and understood its meaning! May our lives and our worship portray the same gratitude, honesty, and sacrifice.

Day 19: Passover

While they were eating, Jesus took bread, gave thanks and broke it, and gave it to his disciples, saying, "Take it; this is my body." Then he took the cup, gave thanks and offered it to them, and they all drank from it. "This is my blood of the covenant, which is poured out for many," he said to them. "I tell you the truth, I will not drink again of the fruit of the vine until that day when I drink it anew in the kingdom of God" (Mark 14:22–26).

The Lord said to Moses and Aaron in Egypt, "This month is to be for you the first month, the first month of your year. Tell the whole community of Israel that on the tenth day of this month each man is to take a lamb for his family, one for each household...Eat it in haste; it is the Lord's Passover. On that same night I will pass through Egypt and strike down every firstborn of both people and an-

imals, and I will bring judgment on all the gods of Egypt. I am the Lord. The blood will be a sign for you on the houses where you are, and when I see the blood, I will pass over you. No destructive plague will touch you when I strike Egypt" (Exodus 12:1–4, 12–13).

Books are to be read from beginning to end, not from the end to beginning. But when it comes to reading and understanding the meaning of the Bible, the Old Testament is best understood from the perspective of the New Testament, which describes what the Old Testament foreshadowed. The interpretive key to the Old Testament's most difficult passages is to recognize that the Bible is a meta-narrative about the Sovereign Lord's redemptive plan as revealed in the New Testament. Notice how the Hebrew Scriptures point us to Jesus:

- When the Lord God prophesied in the garden at the beginning of history that the head of the enemy would be crushed by the offspring of Eve, he was foreshadowing Jesus Christ, who by his death on the cross and his resurrection, would destroy the power of the enemy and reverse the curse.

- Noah emblematized Jesus when he rescued

his family and provided salvation from God's judgment.

- The story of Abraham's willingness to sacrifice his son, Isaac, on Mount Moriah foreshadows another Son who would lay down his life atop another mountain.

- When Moses led the Israelites out of slavery in Egypt into the promised land in Canaan, he was heralding a new and better exodus in the work of Jesus on the cross.

- When the Lord God established the law with Moses, he was pointing to the one who would ultimately fulfill that law with his perfect life.

- The story of Ruth and Naomi, who found a kinsman-redeemer in Boaz, is a precursor of the ultimate redeemer who would rescue us from our impoverished condition and mercifully welcome us into his family.

- The account of Joseph rising from the pit of slavery to sit at the right hand of Egypt's throne, only to offer forgiveness and redemption to those who betrayed him foreshadows the coming of a new and better Joseph.

- As a shepherd boy David defeated Goliath, the hated enemy of Israel, and his victory became the nation's victory. In the same way, Jesus, our good shepherd, destroyed our hated enemy of sin and death, and his victory becomes our victory.

- In Genesis, Jesus is the seed of Eve. In Exodus, he is the Passover lamb. In Leviticus, he is the High Priest. In Numbers, he is the cloud by day and the pillar of fire by night. In Deuteronomy, he is the liberator from slavery. In Joshua, he is the one who leads us to the promised land. In Judges, he is judge and law-giver. In Ruth, he is the kinsman redeemer. In 1 & 2 Samuel, he is our trusted prophet. In Kings & Chronicles, he is our reigning king. In Ezra, he is the faithful scribe.

- In Nehemiah, Jesus is the rebuilder of the wall. In Esther, he is Mordecai. In Job, he is Dayspring. In Psalms, he is the Good Shepherd. In Proverbs, he is our wisdom. In Song of Solomon, he is the bride's lover. In Jeremiah, he is the weeping prophet. In Isaiah, he is the Suffering Servant. In Ezekiel, he is the Son of Man. In Daniel, he is present in the furnace. In Hosea, he is the Lion of Judah. In Joel, he is the Lord who judges.

- In Amos, Jesus is the burden bearer. In Obadiah, he is the mighty Savior. In Jonah, he is merciful salvation. In Micah, he is the messenger with beautiful feet. In Nahum, he is the avenger. In Habakkuk, he is the great evangelist. In Zephaniah, he is the restorer of hope. In Haggai, he is the cleansing fountain. In Zechariah, he is the one they have pierced. In Malachi, Jesus is the son of righteousness.

We find Jesus on every page of the Old Testament Scriptures. All of the Bible points to his redemptive work, nowhere is this more true than with Passover.

The Passover meal, which Jesus and the disciples celebrated before Jesus' death, was an important event for first-century Jews. Passover commemorates the most important story in the Israelites' history and is a central focus of biblical faith. It also plays a central role in Christian worship as "The Lord's Supper." But to understand its meaning, we need to reflect on the actual event that Passover represents.

The word "passover" comes from a story in the book

of Exodus when a death angel "passed over" the homes of the Israelites in Egypt, sparing them God's judgment. The Lord God had inflicted ten plagues on the people of Egypt, each more intense, to induce Pharaoh to liberate the Israelites from bondage. The last and most severe plague was the death angel, sent to claim every first-born child unless the family sacrificed a lamb without blemish and smeared its blood on the doorpost. After the devastation of this final plague, Pharaoh relented, and Israel was set free.

The death angel represents the unleashing of God's perfect justice over humanity. That incredible force moved over the powerful Egyptian nation like a warm knife through butter, bringing death and judgment without bias on every home. Think about the significance of this truth: God told the Israelites that the only thing standing between them and the most powerful force in the universe, the judgment of God, was a helpless little lamb. They were to shed its blood and place it on their doorposts.

Each element of the Passover meal reflects a significant aspect of the Israelites' liberation. The lamb on the table represents the sacrifice. The bitter herbs represent the bitterness of slavery, and the unleavened bread recalls the immediacy of their liberation, so abrupt that they had no time to wait for their bread to rise. The cup of wine is an image of the blood of the lamb shed for their salvation.

How are we to understand the meaning of the Passover meal that would later become the Lord's Supper? What do death angels, divine judgment, and sacrificial lambs have to do with modern people?

As with other images in the Old Testament, the symbolism of Passover explodes with meaning when viewed from the perspective of the cross. Bitter herbs reveal the bitterness of our slavery to sin; broken un-leavened bread reminds us that Jesus was broken for our transgressions to liberate us from the slavery of our sinful condition. The wine reminds us of his blood, shed for our salvation.

This was the meal that Jesus and the disciples shared as he prepared for the cross. He instructed them to continue to celebrate it in commemoration of his redemptive work on the cross. The bread would represent his body broken and the cup the covenant established by his blood.

I've often wondered what the disciples might have been thinking at that last Passover supper. I wonder if they put everything together. Likely enough, they had limited understanding until they could look back on Jesus' words after the resurrection. After they had seen his body broken at the crucifixion, the bread surely took on new meaning. Seeing his blood shed must have brought special meaning to the new covenant represented by the cup.

But I especially wonder what they must have thought about the lamb, or rather, the lack of it. None of the biblical accounts of that last Passover meal includes a lamb on the table. Where was it? Was it merely omitted from the story because it was assumed to have been there? Or could there be another meaning to its absence?

The symbolism of the sacrificial lamb holds particular significance to Jesus' death and resurrection. When Jesus began his earthly ministry, he was baptized by his cousin, John the Baptist, who saw him from a distance and called out:

> *Behold the Lamb of God who takes away the sins of the world!* (John 1:29)

Jesus' instructions for establishing the Lord's Supper did not include adding a lamb to the meal. What can the absence of lamb mean? Perhaps there was no lamb at the table because the perfect lamb without blemish was already sitting at the table.

Day 20: Bread

While they were eating, Jesus took bread, gave thanks and broke it, and gave it to his disciples, saying, "Take it; this is my body" (Mark 14:22).

"This bread is my body broken for you" (1 Corinthians 11:24).

Pastors learn early in ministry that people don't like it when you change a tradition. As a very young pastor, I changed the order of our worship service, moving the offering from the middle of the service to the end. Seems like a simple change, right? Seriously, who would even notice? At least that's what I thought.

But I was young, naïve, and inexperienced. I had not yet discovered one of the unspoken commandments God reveals to pastors as they get a little older: Thou shalt never assume people won't notice when you change a tradition.

It took me about six months to convince some of my church members that the Apostle Paul actually did not take the offering in the middle of the worship. I remember lying awake at night thinking, "If these people are this angry with me about changing the order of service, what will they think of me when I tell them the Apostle Paul didn't use an organ?"

The disciples would have noticed some changes Jesus made to the Passover tradition. For instance, rather than repeating the traditional mantra, "This is the bread of affliction which our fathers ate in the wilderness," as was common, Jesus said:

"This is the bread of MY affliction."

Jesus was implying that the bread symbolized the affliction he would suffer to bring his followers out of a greater bondage—a bondage of sin and death! He was saying, "Years ago the Israelites ate this supper on the night when God brought them out of Pharaoh's bondage, but tonight I'm going to liberate you from sin and death itself."

Jesus replaced the old phrase about the bread with a new phrase that held a mind-boggling implication. The symbols and traditions of the Old Testament faith were being supplanted by a new, amazing reality. The disciples would come to understand that all the symbols of the Passover were fulfilled in Jesus. In fact, the entire Old Testament was fulfilled in him! Paul says this:

For no matter how many promises God has made, they are "yes" in Christ. And so through him the "amen" is spoken by us to the glory of God (2 Corinthians 12:20).

All the promises, symbols, festivals, covenants, and prophecies of the Old Testament find their answer in Jesus Christ. Consider all the meaningful ways Jesus is symbolized in just the bread of the Passover meal.

First, the bread was made without leaven, which is the bread of slaves. Unleavened bread is quickly and cheaply made because it does not need to rise. Called "matzah," the flat, hard bread was easy to store and transport, and was the bread that slaves in Egypt would have been accustomed to eating. As a symbol of freedom from bondage, eating unleavened bread reminded the Jews how God had brought them out of their lowly status as slaves into a new way of life.

Seven days you shall eat unleavened bread, the bread of affliction, for you came out of the land of Egypt in haste—that all the days of your life you may remember the day when

you came out of the land of Egypt (Deuteronomy 16:3).

Second, to celebrate the meal, God told the Israelites
to remove all traces of leaven from their houses
(Exodus 12:5, 13:7; Deuteronomy 16:4). On the night
before Passover, the Jews would perform a ceremony
called "bedicat chametz" in which they removed all
bread crumbs or other traces of bread from their houses.
Why was this important? Leaven (or yeast) produces
fermentation, especially in bread dough, and is the result
of natural processes of decay. Unless it is removed, it can
influence the unleavened dough.

Leavening represents death and decay, and therefore,
Jesus is the symbolic unleavened bread that defeats sin
and death. He rose from the grave and was not overcome
by the power of death.

Third, as with removing all leavening and bread crumbs
from the house, Passover represents a new beginning, a
starting over. God took the Israelites from their Egyptian
bondage to a new way of living. Similarly, in Christ,
we are transformed by the power of the Gospel, and all
things become new:

Therefore, if anyone is in Christ, the new creation
has come: The old has gone, the new is here!
(2 Corinthians 5:17)

Fourth, the matzah was called the "bread of affliction," signifying the hardship of Egyptian slavery. As believers, we recognize a profound symbolism of the bread as the body of Christ, broken for us. He took our sin and death onto himself. He became sin for us and died in our place. Isaiah the prophet wrote:

> *Surely he took up our pain*
> *and bore our suffering,*
> *yet we considered him punished by God,*
> *stricken by him, and afflicted.*
> *But he was pierced for our transgressions,*
> *he was crushed for our iniquities;*
> *the punishment that brought us peace was on him,*
> *and by his wounds we are healed (Isaiah 53:4-5).*

God's grace brought salvation to the ancient Israelites, just as God's grace saves us from our sins. To eat unleavened bread, the "bread of affliction," is to eat the bread of Christ's affliction, and therefore, to testify to our powerlessness to save ourselves. We eat it "in haste," not with human planning or work. The unleavened bread symbolizes that salvation is of the Lord, rather than from human striving.

Jesus regarded the idea that we can merit righteousness before God, that we are self-sufficient and do not need a Savior, as a form of "spiritual leaven" (Mark 16:6-12). Only when we humble ourselves (are unleavened) can we discern the truth of our fallen nature, turn to him for salvation, and be rescued from slavery.

Day 21: Craving

On the first day of the Festival of Unleavened Bread, the disciples came to Jesus and asked, "Where do you want us to make preparations for you to eat the Passover?" (Matthew 26:17)

He satisfies the thirsty and fills the hungry with good things! (Psalm 107:9)

Blessed are those who hunger and thirst for righteousness, for they will be filled (Matthew 5:6).

A conversation about a meal is not complete unless we deal with the issue of craving. After all, that's the purpose of a meal, to do something about appetite.

A poor appetite means something is wrong with the body, and a lack of craving for spiritual food is a sign of an unhealthy soul. Jesus taught that happiness comes from a wholehearted, passionate appetite for righteousness;

merely nibbling around the edges is not enough. C. S. Lewis wrote:

> It would seem that Our Lord finds our desires not too strong, but too weak. We are half-hearted creatures, fooling about with drink and sex and ambition when infinite joy is offered us, like an ignorant child who wants to go on making mud pies in a slum because he cannot imagine what is meant by the offer of a holiday at the sea. We are far too easily pleased.

When the body is deprived of food or water for long periods, a desperate and even dangerous situation develops. David entered the house of God and unlawfully ate the bread of the Presence because he and his men were hungry (1 Samuel 21:6). Thirst also drives men to desperate measures. Ancient Israel's desert with its intense heat and scarce water supply was a place where people understood dehydration.

Years ago a group from our church went on a long hike in the Jordan desert not far from the Dead Sea. Although we thought we had packed plenty of water, our bodies were sapped of hydration more quickly than we had predicted, and our situation became desperate. One of the youngest and strongest in our group was hospitalized with dehydration and symptoms of heat stroke. The experience was a lesson I will never forget!

In his book, *King Solomon's Mines*, H. Rider Haggard told of three men and their guide who ran out of water. The Zulu guide said, "If we cannot find water, we shall all be dead before the moon rises tomorrow." Recalling the torture of thirst and the hallucinations it created, one of the men said:

> *If the Cardinal had been there, with his bell, book, and candle, I would have whipped in and drunk his water up, yea, even if I knew that the whole concentrated curse of the Catholic Church should fall on me for so doing.* (*King Solomon's Mines*, p. 58)

When the body is desperately hungry or thirsty, the mind focuses intently on survival, nothing else. The Psalmist wrote:

> *As the deer pants for streams of water, so my soul pants for you, my God* (Psalm 42:1).

Without hunger or thirst, we will not crave what we need. If the prodigal son had not ended up so hungry that he was willing to eat pig slop, he may never have returned to his father. Hunger drove him to long for home, for a physical feast of rich food, and the spiritual banquet of forgiveness.

Physical hunger is painful, but soul hunger is worse. We learn in our hunger and thirst that nothing can satisfy except for Jesus Christ and his purposes. Anything we try as a substitute for his presence only makes our situation worse. When we are hungry, we need substantive calories; when we are truly thirsty, nothing satisfies like pure water. The Spirit spurs our hunger and thirst, so that our hearts are focused on what is most important and satisfying.

Many people go through life trying to satisfy spiritual hunger and thirst in the wrong way. They look for satisfaction in sex, wealth, power, or popularity—things that can never truly satisfy. You can't get much more popular than Tom Brady. His name is synonymous with NFL football greatness. He is on the top of the heap when it comes to pro quarterbacks. He has been the field general of the most successful team in the most popular sport in America over the past ten years. He is a mega-multimillionaire who has won four Super Bowl titles, three MVPs, thirteen division titles, has a supermodel wife, and legendary pop culture status. He is wealthy, good-looking, athletic, and smart. Tom Brady is the poster child for the American dream. Who could want anything more? If wealth, popularity, and status are the measure of ultimate fulfillment in life, then no one on earth should be more satisfied than Tom Brady. Except he isn't. In an interview on *60 Minutes* in June 2005, Brady reflectively asked this question:

> *Why do I have four Super Bowl rings and still think there's something greater out there for me? I think it's got to be more than this. I mean, this isn't it. This can't be what it's all cracked up to be. I wish I knew the answer.*

Brady's question is a common one from those who've made it to the top: "Is this all there is?" Sadly, some people climb the ladder of success only to find it is leaning against the wrong building. They try to satisfy their inner hunger and thirst in the wrong ways. Consider the Samaritan woman whom Jesus met at a well as she was drawing water. Jesus somehow knew that the woman's life was tangled in multiple destructive relationships, and so he drew a comparison between her physical thirst and her spiritual thirst:

> *Whoever drinks the water I give them will never thirst. Indeed, the water I give them will become in them a spring of water welling up to eternal life* (John 4:13).

The meaning of the Lord's Supper reminds us that our

true thirst can be satisfied only in the well Christ offers. We must feast on the knowledge of the unrelenting love that sent Jesus to the cross, broken and spilled out, dying in our place.

Spiritual hunger reveals the need for true life and meaning, proves our need for spiritual fullness, which is a life made possible by Christ on the cross. Through the Holy Spirit, we are shaped in the image of Christ and possess qualities of love, joy, peace, patience, kindness, goodness, gentleness, faithfulness, and self-control (Galatians 5:22–23). The strength and frequency of our hunger awakens our spiritual nature within, and we know our lives need proper nourishment, which comes from studying his word. Jesus said:

> *Man shall not live on bread alone, but on every word that comes from the mouth of God* (Matthew 4:5).

The natural craving of the soul fixates on what it needs most and will not be satisfied by substitutes. We may try other things, but our hearts long for Christ. As the natural body must be fed several times a day, so must the soul be fed regularly to be made alive in Christ. Therefore, Jesus is "the bread of life," the food of the soul most frequently necessary. He is the "fountain of life" because he is the only one who can truly satisfy our longing.

Christianity is about a banquet and a bath. We celebrate the ordinances of baptism and the Lord's Supper as a way of commemorating this important truth: Christ cleanses us by his blood and his atoning sacrifice and invites us to the banquet to celebrate his thirst-quenching, hunger-satisfying presence in our lives.

Day 22: Cup

In the same way, after supper he took the cup, saying, "This cup is the new covenant in my blood; do this, whenever you drink it, in remembrance of me" (1 Corinthians 11:25).

Jesus started a new tradition at the Passover meal when he lifted a cup and said, "This cup is the new covenant in my blood."

Interestingly, there is no mention of a cup in God's instructions regarding the Passover meal in Exodus 12, although Jewish tradition would later include four cups of wine representing the four blessings and curses of Moses' confrontation with Pharaoh. So what is the historical meaning of the cup Jesus lifted to the disciples at that first Lord's Supper?

The Hebrew Scriptures provide some clues. Throughout the Old Testament the cup is a symbol of

God's judgment: the cup of fury, the cup of judgment, the cup of trembling, and the cup of horror and desolation. The cup carries an image of the righteousness and justice of God. (To ancient people, the cup also carried the connotation of execution. Recall that Socrates was sentenced to die by drinking a cup of poison.) Although none of these Old Testament references to the cup have to do with Passover, the theme of God's judgment figures dramatically in the image of the death angel. Only the blood of the lamb on their doorposts rescued God's people from that judgment.

In the Passover tradition, the wine in the cup was an image of that blood. No doubt Jesus was thinking about the cup of God's judgment when he held up the cup and declared a new covenant in his blood.

A covenant, which signifies a renewed relationship between God and his people, is an important concept in Scripture. Here are four examples from the Old Testament:

- God established a covenant with Noah when he said, "I establish my covenant with you, that never again shall all flesh be cut off by the waters of the flood, and never again shall there be a flood to destroy the earth" (Genesis 9:11).

- He established a covenant with Abraham saying, "Now the Lord had said to Abram: 'Get out of your country, from your family and from your father's house, to a land that I will show you. I will make you a great nation; I will bless you and make your name great; and you shall be a blessing. I will bless those who bless you, and I will curse him who curses you; and in you all the families of the earth shall be blessed'" (Genesis 12:1–3).

- The Lord God also made a covenant with Moses when he said, "'Now therefore, if you will indeed obey My voice and keep My covenant, then you shall be a special treasure to Me above all people; for all the earth is Mine. And you shall be to Me a kingdom of priests and a holy nation.' These are the words which you shall speak to the children of Israel" (Exodus 19:5–6).

- He established a covenant with David this way: "When your days are fulfilled and you lie down with your fathers, I will raise up your offspring after you, who shall come from your body, and I will establish his kingdom. He shall build a house for my name, and I will establish the throne of his kingdom forever. I will be to him a father, and he shall be to me a son" (2 Samuel 7:12–17).

The story of the Old Testament is the story of how the people of God tried and failed to live up to the many covenants God established with them. These failures through hundreds of years of biblical history were painstakingly recorded to dramatically illustrate that truth. In other words, all these covenants point to a new and better day when the Messiah, whom the prophets foretold, would usher in a new kingdom and a new, eternal relationship between God and his people. The prophet Jeremiah announced a new covenant that the Lord God would bring about to fulfill all the old covenants and usher in this future kingdom:

> *"This is the covenant I will make with the people of Israel after that time," declares the LORD. "I will put my law in their minds and write it on their hearts. I will be their God, and they will be my people. No longer will they teach their neighbor, or say to one another, 'Know the LORD,' because they will all know me, from the least of them to the greatest," declares the LORD. "For I will forgive their wickedness and will remember their sins no more"* (Jeremiah 31:33–34).

In the new covenant, God pledges to forgive the people's sins and to write his laws not on stone tablets, but within their hearts. Gone are the days when God's people are held to covenants they are incapable of keeping. With the new covenant, God says: "All of it will fall on me, I will create in you the establishment of a new power!"

The new covenant is not a mere possibility; it is a new creation. It is not something God proposes, but something he accomplishes. It is the creation of a people for God who will not forsake him. They will be his people, and he will be their God forever. The certainty of it lies not in them, but in God's covenant commitment: He says that he forgives their sin and remembers their iniquity no more.

We find another promise of the new covenant declared by Moses in Deuteronomy 30:6:

> *And the Lord your God will circumcise your heart and the heart of your offspring, so that you will love the Lord your God with all your heart and with all your soul, that you may live.*

In the new covenant, "Thou shalt love the Lord your God" is not only a command, but also a gift. Ezekiel 36:27 describes God's new covenant commitment like this:

I will put my Spirit within you and cause you to walk in my statutes and be careful to observe my ordinances.

In the new arrangement, our position before God is not in question—God secures it with the blood of Christ and with the infinite power of his Spirit. The connection between the new covenant, the death of Christ, and God's Spirit in our lives is clear in Hebrews 13:20–21:

Now may the God of peace who brought again from the dead our Lord Jesus, the great shepherd of the sheep by the blood of the eternal covenant, equip you with everything good that you may do his will, working in you that which is pleasing in his sight, through Jesus Christ; to whom be glory for ever and ever. Amen.

As you can see, this new covenant was a game changer of eternal proportions! In fact, it was what the entire Old Testament pointed toward in hundreds of years of Israelite history. The new covenant is what the Passover meal foreshadowed with the imagery of a lamb slain for the salvation of God's people and with the symbolism of the bread of affliction.

This is why Jesus' statement about the cup is so powerfully significant. With his statement, "This cup is the NEW COVENANT in my blood," Jesus announced an amazing and powerful new reality available to all of us. Then, in the Garden of Gethsemane, Jesus cried out to the Lord in anguished prayer:

> *"Father, if it is Your will, take this cup away from me; nevertheless not my will, but yours, be done"* (Luke 22:42).

The next time you hold the cup at a Lord's Supper meal, remember that Jesus took the cup of wrath and drank it to the dregs so that you could drink from the cup of blessing. Remember that because of his blood shed on the cross, a new covenant was established.

Day 23: Communion

In the following directives I have no praise for you, for your meetings do more harm than good. In the first place, I hear that when you come together as a church, there are divisions among you, and to some extent I believe it. No doubt there have to be differences among you to show which of you have God's approval. So then, when you come together, it is not the Lord's Supper you eat, for when you are eating, some of you go ahead with your own private suppers. As a result, one person remains hungry and another gets drunk. Don't you have homes to eat and drink in? Or do you despise the church of God by humiliating those who have nothing? What shall I say to you? Shall I praise you? Certainly not in this matter! (1 Corinthians 11:17–22)

In the past few years, sociologists and psychologists

have talked a lot about challenging new problems in human society brought about by the Internet and social media. People are becoming more isolated even as they become more connected. In his book, *Bowling Alone*, Robert Putnam made the point that the greatest social epidemic in American life is loneliness. What is the solution? Many have suggested that families get back to doing something that has been part of daily life for centuries: eating together.

What a radical idea!

Many families today eat on the run, scarfing down fast-food meals extracted from drive-through windows and passed to the back seats of minivans. We tend to hurry through meals as if they were a necessary evil. Teenagers often eat alone in front of computers or video games with headphones blaring.

The average American eats one in five meals in the car. One in four Americans eats at least one fast-food meal every single day, and the majority of American families report eating a single meal together fewer than five days a week. How sad that so many Americans are missing out on what could be a meaningful time with their loved ones! But what's more, eating alone also has quantifiably negative physical and psychological effects.

Using data from nearly three-quarters of the world's countries, the Organization for Economic Cooperation and Development (OECD) found that students who did not regularly eat with their parents were significantly more likely to have problems in school and to experience emotional and physical health problems.

In her book, *Eating Together*, Alice Julier argued that having a meal together can radically shift one's point of view: "It reduces people's perceptions of inequality, and participants tend to view those of different races, genders, and socioeconomic backgrounds as more equal than they would in other social scenarios."

We Christians know that the idea of sharing a meal is not new. Jesus told us to eat together in the normal flow of life within the body of Christ. He instructed his church to come together occasionally and have a meal to commemorate his death. Not only is the Lord's Supper important as a time to remember his sacrifice on the cross for our sins, but also as a shared experience. The Lord's Supper is a remembrance and a fellowship, and both are essential to the celebration.

The first Lord's Supper was not a stoic event in which people stared straight ahead and quietly received the bread and cup. There were feet being washed, heart-felt conversations, and deep expressions of community.

The disciples looked each other in the eye, talked with one another, and had fellowship. In other words, the community they shared together was as significant as the remembrance.

As technological advances and busy schedules increasingly fracture our culture into isolation and loneliness, I sense an even greater importance for the church to uphold not just the symbolism of the Lord's Supper, but also its fellowship. People crave community, and the church should meet that need and show the way.

In 1 Corinthians 11, Paul criticized church members for their divisions over how communion should be received. The church was playing favorites, and many were feeling left out during fellowship meals. The wealthy were getting plenty to eat while the poor were forgotten, which Paul pointed out was an insult to the body of Christ! A church is a place where everyone has a seat at the table and is loved equally without prejudice. The very word "communion" means "common union." Paul made it clear that one of the most important aspects of church life is that we are in it together, loving each other equally. He linked the communion meal to the importance of living in community.

God wants community for us. The Scripture is clear: If we want to experience God's presence, we must seek him through his word, through the power of his Holy Spirit, and through our relationships. More often than not, the way you hear God speak is from conversations with God's people, because he lives inside those who love him. God wants to help you in your life. He wants to speak to you. But most likely he will not write on a wall or send an angel to appear before you. Instead, he will reveal himself in a meaningful conversation with a brother or a sister in Christ. Jesus said:

> *A new command I give you: Love one another. As I have loved you, so you must love one another. By this everyone will know that you are my disciples, if you love one another* (John 13:34–35).

That command may be more relevant today than ever. There are two important take-aways in the Lord's Supper: Remember what Jesus did for you and enjoy each other more.

Sunday Reflection:
The Passover Meal

Read John 12:1–11; Matthew 26:1–29; Mark 14:22–26.

1. What does the story of Mary washing Jesus' feet teach us about the meaning of worship?

2. How did Judas get it wrong?

3. What is Passover?

4. How does Passover point us to Jesus?

5. In what ways does the blood of Jesus keep us from God's judgment?

6. Why is the Lord's Supper important to the believer?

Week Four: The Passover Meal

Week Five: Garden of Gethsemane

Matthew 26:36–46

Day 24: Pressure

Then Jesus went with his disciples to a place called Gethsemane, and he said to them, "Sit here while I go over there and pray." He took Peter and the two sons of Zebedee along with him, and he began to be sorrowful and troubled. Then he said to them, "My soul is overwhelmed with sorrow to the point of death. Stay here and keep watch with me." Going a little farther, he fell with his face to the ground and prayed, "My Father, if it is possible, may this cup be taken from me. Yet not as I will, but as you will." Then he returned to his disciples and found them sleeping. "Couldn't you men keep watch with me for one hour?" he asked Peter. "Watch and pray so that you will not fall into temptation. The spirit is willing, but the flesh is weak." He went away a second time and prayed, "My Father, if it is not possible for this cup to be taken away unless I drink it, may your

*will be done." When he came back, he again
found them sleeping, because their eyes were
heavy. So he left them and went away once
more and prayed the third time, saying the
same thing. Then he returned to the disciples
and said to them, "Are you still sleeping and
resting? Look, the hour has come, and the Son
of Man is delivered into the hands of sinners.
Rise! Let us go! Here comes my betrayer!"*
(Matthew 26:36–46)

On the way to the cross, Jesus took the disciples to
Gethsemane, a garden of olive trees perched on the side
of the Mount of Olives. The Bible says Jesus experienced excruciating emotions while in the garden. He
asked his disciples to stay and pray with him. He was
feeling the weight of the universe in those moments. He
knew the eternal significance of what he had to do. In
his humanity, he wished the cup could be removed from
him, but in his divine nature, he was determined to carry
it through. The weight of those two opposing pressures
bore down on his heart relentlessly.

The garden was a place of intense emotional
struggle. Interestingly, even the name denotes pressure.
"Gethsemane," an English corruption of the two Hebrew
words, GAT and SHMANIM, literally means "the place
where olive oil is pressed."

Hebrews 12 tells us that Jesus, because of the joy set before him, "endured the cross, scorning its shame." In other words, while under immense torment and suffering, Jesus pressed on and accomplished the task he knew he had to accomplish. How did Jesus handle this enormous pressure?

The first thing to notice is that Jesus established a singular priority for his life: to do the work he was called to do. He began his ministry saying, "I must be about my father's business," and he ended it saying, "It is finished." The lesson is that no matter how much pressure we may be under in life, we must keep our focus on those things that are most important.

The pressure and stress we experience in this life often comes from worrying about things that really don't matter all that much. The title of Richard Carlson's book, *Don't Sweat the Small Stuff and It's All Small Stuff*, says it all: Most things we worry about in this life are of very little eternal significance and not worth the time and energy it takes to stress about them. Jesus said:

> *Do not worry about your life, what you will eat or drink; or about your body, what you will wear. Is not life more than food, and the body more than clothes? Look at the birds of the air; they do not sow or reap or*

store away in barns, and yet your heavenly Father feeds them. Are you not much more valuable than they? Can any one of you by worrying add a single hour to your life? (Matthew 6:25–27)

Then, he said this:

But seek first his kingdom and his righteousness, and all these things will be given to you as well (Matthew 6:33).

The next time a particular issue in your life has you feeling overwhelmed with worry and stress, ask yourself: "Does this really matter in the eternal scheme of things?" Most of the stuff we worry about won't matter a year from now or ten years from now, much less in eternity! One of the keys to getting through life's pressures is to focus your heart on those things that are eternally important, such as loving God with your whole heart and loving others as yourself. The other less substantive worries that come into your life, Jesus says, will take care of themselves.

The second way that Jesus handled the pressure of Gethsemane is that he gave all of his worries over to the sovereign will of God. Worry is negative meditation, while prayer is positive meditation. When we feel pressure, we can meditate in a negative way, which only brings us down, or in a positive way as we turn our worries over to God's sovereign will, which lifts us up.

When I look at my life and my problems from the perspective of God's work in eternity, they seem much smaller. Often we cannot change our circumstances, but we can always change our perspective about those circumstances.

Even Jesus spent time in prayer when he was under pressure. The Bible teaches us:

> *Do not be anxious about anything, but in everything by prayer and supplication with thanksgiving let your requests be made known to God. And the peace of God, which surpasses all understanding, will guard your hearts and your minds in Christ Jesus* (Philippians 2:6–7).

The reason God wants us to pray is not because our prayers give him more information, but because our prayers change the way we think. Prayer changes the heart of the person praying! So how should we pray? Prayer is aligning our will to the will of God, and the best way to do that is through the promises of Scripture. One of the most important things we can do when under stress is to talk positively to ourselves, reminding our hearts of what is most important by meditating on God's word. Prayerful meditation focuses our hearts on God's promises.

> *Why, my soul, are you downcast? Why so dis-*
> *turbed within me? Put your hope in God, for*
> *I will yet praise him, my Savior and my God*
> (Psalm 43:5).

In this verse, the psalmist converses with his own soul, reminding himself of God's promises. There will be times in our lives when we will feel as if the weight of the universe is on our shoulders. In those times, remember that only one person ever literally carried the weight of the world, and even he spent time in fervent prayer where he found God's purposes and promises. That is how we can get through life's inevitable pressures as well.

Day 25: Friendship

He took Peter and the two sons of Zebedee along with him, and he began to be sorrowful and troubled. Then he said to them, "My soul is overwhelmed with sorrow to the point of death. Stay here and keep watch with me" (Matthew 26:37).

In his agony in the garden, Jesus asked his closest friends to come around him and pray for him. His desire for their fellowship is a beautiful picture of the humanity of Jesus at a time of deep sorrow. All human beings need friendship. It is one of the strongest, most important longings of the human condition. True friendship multiplies our joys and divides our sorrows. Our friendships make us stronger and encourages us. More than just about any other influence in life, our friendships shape our character. "As iron sharpens iron, so one man sharpens another" (Proverbs 27:17), the Bible says. If you want to know what you will be like ten years from now, look at your friends—they are the ones who are "sharpening" you.

I can't stress enough the importance of cultivating strong, meaningful, Christian friendships. Aside from our relationship with God, these relationships may be the single most important determinant of our spiritual growth.

As I read and meditate on the passage about Jesus in the garden with James, John, and Peter, I can't help but think what an enormous privilege it must have been to be in that tight circle of friendship. Yet, Jesus invites each and every one of us into his friendship circle:

> *I no longer call you servants, because a servant does not know his master's business. Instead, I have called you friends, for everything that I learned from my Father I have made known to you* (John 15:15).

The thought that we can be a friend of God seems like a pretty radical idea. What does it mean? It means our priorities must change to make room for his friendship. The key is to decide what we want more in life, friendship with God or friendship with the world. No one has time to be friends with everybody, so we have to be selective and discerning. Friendship takes a commitment of time and energy. To be in friendship with God, we have to make our relationship with him a priority.

The Bible says:

> *Some of these people have missed the most important thing in life—they don't know God* (1 Timothy 6:21, The Living Bible).

We may know our fantasy league stats, the stock market, the latest pop stars, or top movies, but if we don't know God, we are missing what is most important in life! The truth is, if we are not a friend of God, then we care about something else more than knowing him. Look at this verse in the Book of James:

> *Don't you know that friendship with the world means enmity against God? Therefore, anyone who chooses to be a friend of the world becomes an enemy of God. Or do you think Scripture says without reason that he jealously longs for the spirit he has caused to dwell in us?* (James 4:4–6)

When James writes "friend of the world," he means loving the world's value system. God wants us to love people in the world, but that doesn't mean loving the world's values. We get so caught up in our busy lifestyles that we tend to do just the opposite. We love the world's value system and forget to love people. We love things. We love pleasure. We love comfort. We love status. We love thrills. We love power and possessions. All of these things are what the world values.

But God loves people, and he wants us to love them, too. We love people by loving what God has created in them and loving them for who they are. We love them by wanting what's best for them.

To be a friend of God means to align our priorities with his priorities and to care about the things that matter to God. God doesn't care about our image, our status, or our circumstances. God cares only about our character, because that is what will last into eternity.

To be a friend of God means to value the very same things that God values and to love the very same things that God loves. I love what Oswald Chambers said in *My Utmost for His Highest* about being a friend of God:

> *Friendship with God means being so intimately in touch with God that you never even need to ask Him to show you His will. It is evidence of a level of intimacy which confirms that you are nearing the final stage of your discipline in the life of faith. When you have a right-standing relationship with*

God, you have a life of freedom, liberty, and delight; you are God's will. And all of your commonsense decisions are actually His will for you, unless you sense a feeling of restraint brought on by a check in your spirit. You are free to make decisions in the light of a perfect and delightful friendship with God, knowing that if your decisions are wrong He will lovingly produce that sense of restraint. Once he does, you must stop immediately.

Friendship with God will never disappoint. In the garden, Jesus modeled true friendship. Under the most crushing weight, he asked his friends for a little support and found they could not stay awake. They left him alone completely, but what did he say? *"The spirit is willing, but the flesh is weak"* (Matthew 26: 41). Isn't that amazing? As he continued to focus on the blessings of the friendship, his response was: "You let me down when I needed it most, but I know you were really trying hard."

In the biggest struggle of his life, Jesus still affirmed the positives he saw in his friends. His lesson for us is that friendship requires large doses of both forgiveness and celebration. When we can forgive the disappointments and celebrate the positives, our friendships will always be strong.

Having loved his own who were in the world, he loved them to the end (John 13:1).

Day 26: Obedience

They went to a place called Gethsemane, and Jesus said to his disciples, "Sit here while I pray." He took Peter, James and John along with him, and he began to be deeply distressed and troubled. "My soul is overwhelmed with sorrow to the point of death," he said to them. "Stay here and keep watch." Going a little farther, he fell to the ground and prayed that if possible the hour might pass from him. "Abba, Father," he said, "everything is possible for you. Take this cup from me. Yet not what I will, but what you will." Then he returned to his disciples and found them sleeping. "Simon," he said to Peter, "are you asleep? Couldn't you keep watch for one hour? Watch and pray so that you will not fall into temptation. The spirit is willing, but the flesh is weak" (Mark 14:32–38).

Most people familiar with the story of Jesus in the Garden of Gethsemane focus more on the failure of the disciples than on the suffering of Jesus. Many sermons have been preached about the inability of Jesus' friends to remain with him when he needed them the most. "Couldn't you keep watch for even an hour?" is a key line in this narrative. But I want us to focus on something many people miss in this story: the unusual intensity of Jesus' agony.

Three of the four Gospel writers, Matthew, Mark and Luke, all make a strong point that the agony of Jesus was uncommonly severe, even more than might be expected. At one point Jesus said, "My sorrow is overwhelming to the point of death." That statement seems to indicate that Jesus was under so much pressure at that moment that he thought it might even physically kill him.

Of course, we have to believe that Jesus Christ in his pre-existent form would have known about the suffering that he would endure on the cross. In fact, the Gospels contain many examples of Jesus telling the disciples that he must suffer and die. So, the knowledge of that suffering would not have been a surprise to him. The question is: What was revealed to Jesus in those moments that became so shockingly disturbing to him that his sorrow nearly overwhelmed him? What changed in his heart so suddenly that caused these emotions?

Matthew 26:37 indicates that Jesus suddenly felt over-whelming sorrow as he and James, John, and Peter walked away from the other disciples. This change happened while he was enroute, as if descending upon him in real time. Not only did Jesus think the sorrow would kill him, but in Mark's account, Jesus was surprised by his emotions. Mark uses the Greek word ekthambeisthai, which means to be moved to an *"intense emotional state because of something causing great surprise or perplexity"* (Walter Bauer, *Greek English Lexicon*).

Many translators translate that phrase as "deeply distressed," probably because they are assuming that as deity, Jesus surely would not have felt a kind of surprised anxiety. But there may be another explanation: I believe that in that moment Jesus saw the true agony he would experience as the Father turned his face from him and the burden of the world's sin came upon him. I believe the cold reality of that loss of eternal fellowship was suddenly revealed to Jesus. In that moment, he truly understood the horrible, brutal consequences of taking on the sins of world. The true agony of Jesus on the cross was not physical suffering, but the separation from God.

Keep in mind that the Gospel writers would have known by this time the many examples of Christians who had faced execution and experienced something dramatically different from what Jesus experienced.

Steven the Martyr, for example, faced that moment and Heaven opened up to him in a glorious way. The Bible says his *"face was like the face of an angel"* (Acts 6:15).

No one ever experienced what Jesus experienced. Jesus certainly knew he would be crucified, but until that moment, he had not fully comprehended the cold reality of taking on the cumulative punishment of all humanity for all eternity. Jesus' sorrow was not caused by fear or a lack of desire to accomplish the task. Rather, Jesus had expected to spend time with God in prayer in the garden, and instead he experienced something shockingly painful to him—the alienation that comes from our sinful condition. Entering into the presence of God, he expected heaven, but hell opened up instead. Jonathan Edwards makes this point in his sermon, "Christ's Agony":

> *The agony of Jesus Christ was caused by a vivid, bright, full, immediate view of the wrath of God. God the Father, as it were, set the cup down before him, which was vastly more terrible than Nebuchadnezzar's furnace.*

Several weeks ago, Teri and I went on a long hike up Mount Princeton outside Buena Vista, Colorado, with some close friends. The hike turned out to be much more difficult than we had anticipated. For most of the final ascent, we climbed over loose boulders. All of us agreed that had we known how difficult the hike would be, we probably would not have tried it. We started out excited to give it a try, but our enthusiasm faded in the experience. What if the night before our hike the reality of the difficulty of the climb had somehow been vividly revealed to us? I doubt we would have gone.

Jesus experienced in the garden a full realization of the dreadful consequences of drinking the cup of wrath. He was given an excruciatingly vivid view, and it staggered him.

And then, he obediently drank it anyway.

Day 27: Grief

Jesus went out as usual to the Mount of Olives, and his disciples followed him. On reaching the place, he said to them, "Pray that you will not fall into temptation." He withdrew about a stone's throw beyond them, knelt down and prayed, "Father, if you are willing, take this cup from me; yet not my will, but yours be done." An angel from heaven appeared to him and strengthened him. And being in anguish, he prayed more earnestly, and his sweat was like drops of blood falling to the ground. When he rose from prayer and went back to the disciples, he found them asleep, exhausted from sorrow. "Why are you sleeping?" he asked them. "Get up and pray so that you will not fall into temptation" (Luke 22:39–46).

Every person who is reading this right now will have

to deal with grief at some point in life. Someday things are going to get difficult, and the bottom will fall out, if it hasn't already. Experiencing grief is a normal part of life. None of us is exempt.

Not even Jesus.

At the Garden of Gethsemane, Jesus experienced the worst day of his life and demonstrated how to get through grief. The Bible says:

> *To this you were called, because Christ suffered for you, leaving you an example, that you should follow in his steps* (1 Peter 2:21).

In his grief, Jesus set a wonderful example on the worst, most painful day of his life on earth. He reached around, and he reached up.

First, he reached around to friends. On the night Jesus knew that he would be arrested, tortured, and executed, he gathered his closest friends around him and asked them to pray with him. He wasn't looking for explanations, advice, or speeches; he simply wanted them to be with him in prayer.

When I was in seminary, my pastoral care professor invited a woman who had tragically lost a son years before to come to our class and talk about her grief. Our conversation with this grieving mother that day was enormously helpful to me. The class full of young ministers spent the entire hour asking her questions about what helped her endure her suffering.

I will never forget her answer to the question, "Was there anything anyone said to you during this time that helped you?" She thought about it several seconds and then answered, "Actually, no, there was nothing anyone could say that could bring me comfort. The only thing that really helped me was close friends insisting to come and sit with me." In my years of ministry after seminary, I have discovered the truth in her words. The most helpful comfort to people in grief is not many words, but loving presence.

When we are in grief, we need people around us, although we do not tend to seek them out. Our instinct is to withdraw and to be alone. But God never meant for us to go through our grief alone. The grieving process cannot be rushed, and truthfully, complete healing will not occur until we get to heaven someday, but a community of people will help. A strong circle of friends who can reach around us and help during grief is very important. In Romans 12:15, Paul tells us to "weep with those who weep." Healing is facilitated when we share our grief with others.

When you are grieving, lean on people around you. Tell them what you need, even if you just need them to be in the same room with you for a couple of hours. Let God use others to comfort you. The Bible says:

> *Two are better than one, because they have a good return for their labor:*
> *If either of them falls down,*
> *one can help the other up.*
> *But pity anyone who falls*
> *and has no one to help them up.*
> *Also, if two lie down together, they will keep warm.*
> *But how can one keep warm alone?*
> *Though one may be overpowered,*
> *two can defend themselves.*
> *A cord of three strands is not quickly broken*
> (Ecclesiastes 4:9–12).

The second thing Jesus did when he was grieving was to reach out to God through prayer. We need friends in times of trouble, but we need God even more. God's love is different than any other—it is unconditional and unmerited. God understands what we need most, and he can handle our honest questions and feelings of disappointment. We can lean on God in our pain through our prayers.

Find your strength in the Lord. If you don't know how to

pray while you are grieving, pray through Scripture. The Psalms are especially helpful. Here are two examples:

> *Turn to me and be gracious to me,*
> *For I am lonely and afflicted.*
> *The troubles of my heart are enlarged;*
> *Bring me out of my distresses.*
> *Look upon my affliction and my trouble,*
> *And forgive all my sins* (Psalm 25:16–18).

> *The righteous cry, and the Lord hears*
> *And delivers them out of all their troubles.*
> *The LORD is near to the brokenhearted*
> *And saves those who are crushed in spirit*
> (Psalm 34:17–18).

The way Jesus prayed in the garden is a great model for how we should pray:

Jesus confessed his true feelings. He said, "Father, if you are willing, take this cup from me." God can handle it when we are truthful with him and express our doubts and weaknesses. When we confess how we truly feel and honestly seek him, God will help us grow into an eternal perspective.

Jesus acknowledged God's power. In his prayer, Jesus affirmed that the Lord God has all power over circumstances. We, too, should acknowledge that God is sovereign and all powerful when we pray. As hurtful as life becomes, God knows what he is doing within the scope of his eternal plan.

Jesus submitted to God by saying "not my will, but yours." God's ways are not always our ways and he knows what's best for us, even when we don't like it. Remember, we don't know the whole picture, and we cannot see our lives from God's perspective. With our limited viewpoint, we can pray: "Lord God, give me all those things I would ask for if I knew what you know."

Day 28: Olive

And if the root be holy, the branches are also.
But if some of the branches were broken off,
and you, being a wild olive were grafted in
among them and became partaker with them
of the root of the fatness of the olive tree
(Romans 11:16–17).

Amazingly, Gethsemane has been preserved for more than 2,000 years, and visitors to the Mount of Olives overlooking Jerusalem can go there today. Carbon dating has shown that many of the trees there are more than a thousand years old, and are believed to be shoots from the trees that Jesus and the disciples sat under that fateful night.

The olive tree is unusual in that even if it is cut all the way to the ground, new life will spring from its roots. Today on the Mount of Olives, ancient olive trees in that sacred spot stand as witnesses to one of the most important events in Christianity—the prayer of Jesus before his arrest.

But the olive tree is also remarkable for symbolic reasons. Ancient Israel considered the olive tree to have semi-sacramental value along with grape vines and wheat grain, items symbolizing abundance and blessing in biblical texts. Bread, wine, and oil all carry powerful imagery in the Hebrew Scriptures and traditions.

As Christians, we can see a clear association with the trinity in this symbolism. Bread is associated with priest-hood and the Word (the Son), wine with kingship and rule (the Father), and olive oil with anointing and God's presence (the Spirit).

The olive tree was the first plant to grow after the flood, and the dove brought an olive branch to Noah to signify God's salvation (Genesis 8). The prophet Zechariah saw two cherubim as two olive trees, feeding the oil of the Spirit into the lampstand of Israel's witness (see Zechariah 4).

The olive has a particular association with guarding God's holiness, and with the Holy of Holies in the Temple, which was guarded by the olive. Two large cherubim of olive wood stood next to the Ark in the Temple, and the doors leading into the Holy of Holies were of olive wood. The doorposts of both the Holy of Holies and the Holy Place were of olive wood (1 Kings 6:23–34). The temple was a virtual olive grove! This is why the Psalmist said:

> *But I am like an olive tree flourishing in the house of God; I trust in God's unfailing love for ever and ever (*Psalm 52:8).

I like to think this was one of the Psalms Jesus meditated on the night of his arrest, as he sat in the holy presence of the Father surrounded by olive trees in that place called Gethsemane.

Day 29: Endurance

Then he returned to the disciples and said to them, "Are you still sleeping and resting? Look, the hour has come, and the Son of Man is delivered into the hands of sinners. Rise! Let us go! Here comes my betrayer!" (Matthew 26:31-46)

Do you remember that story about a commencement address Winston Churchill gave in which he said three words, "Never give up!" and then sat down? Great story, right? Well, it never happened. At least the part about him saying only those three words. I really wish it had happened because it's a great story, and there is great truth in those simple words: No matter what happens in life, NEVER GIVE UP. Emphasizing just those three words would have been a stroke of genius.

I was disappointed to learn that Churchill's three-word speech never happened, especially since I'd heard the story many times through the years. However, an actual speech Great Britain's famous prime minister gave on October 29, 1941, at Harrow School in London did contain something like those three words, and the rest of what he said is worth reading:

Never give in, never give in, never, never, never, never—in nothing, great or small, large or petty—never give in except to convictions of honour and good sense. Never yield to force; never yield to the apparently overwhelming might of the enemy. We stood all alone a year ago, and to many countries it seemed that our account was closed, we were finished. All this tradition of ours, our songs, our school history, this part of the history of this country, were gone and finished and liquidated. Very different is the mood today. Britain, other nations thought, had drawn a sponge across her slate. But instead our country stood in the gap. There was no flinching and no thought of giving in; and by what seemed almost a miracle to those outside these islands, though we ourselves never doubted it, we now find ourselves in a position where I say that we can be sure that we have only to persevere to conquer.

There is great truth in those words! People who persevere, who are faithful to the end, are typically the ones who succeed in life. When the going gets tough, most people quit, but the ones who never give in—never, never, never in things great or small—are the ones who are the most successful. The champion is not the one who never gets knocked down; the champion is the one who keeps getting up and never quits.

Maybe today you feel like giving up. Maybe you are telling yourself you don't have the energy, the passion, the desire to keep going. Today is a good day for you to think of Jesus in Gethsemane in his darkest hour. Meditate on the truth that God's love has never given up on you.

All of Jesus' earthly life was moving toward one eventuality in the garden that night. All of history was culminating to this one event: Jesus was about to be arrested and executed. The soldiers and temple guards were bearing down on the garden in the dead of night to arrest him in secret. He knew they were coming. He had prepared and planned for this, his final hour. In football terms, he was at the two-minute warning at the end of the fourth quarter. He could hear them coming in the distance.

This would have been the time for Jesus to quit. He

could have called 10,000 angels if he had wanted, or with one word he could end it. But in John 10:17–18 he said, *"No one takes my life from me; I lay it down of myself."* Jesus could have easily said, "I quit." But Jesus never gave up.

What caused Christ to persevere to the end? Romans 5:8 says that Christ died for us because he loves us. Jesus said the greatest love is the kind that is willing to die for others (John 15:13). The Bible says that God so loved the world that he gave his only son (John 3:16). Jesus persevered because of his love. Paul wrote an entire chapter on love, 1 Corinthians 13, and said this in verse 7:

> *Love always protects, always trusts, always hopes, always perseveres. Love never fails.*

God's love always perseveres. It never fails you. Jesus endured to the end because of his love for you and me.

In Luke 15, we read three parables that Jesus told to illustrate the love of God: The shepherd who would not quit until he found a lost sheep; the housewife who would not quit until she found a lost coin; and a father's love endured well past the time his lost son was restored to him. All three stories revealed one powerful and important truth about God's great love for us: God pursues us relentlessly and never gives up. That's what love does—it always perseveres.

Lee Ielpi understands the meaning of this kind of love. A New York City firefighter, Ielpi retired after twenty-six years of service to his community. But on September 11, 2001, he gave something much more precious: He lost a son in the terrorist attack on the World Trade Center. His son, Jonathan Ielpi, was one of the firefighters who was racing to the top of one of the towers when the building crashed to the ground, trapping his body under tons of concrete and steel.

According to tradition, no one is allowed to touch the body of a firefighter who perishes in the line of duty until a close friend or family member is able to carry the body away. Lee was determined to be the one to carry his son out of that monstrous wreckage. For three weeks, he worked relentlessly with his fellow firefighters at that sixteen-acre graveyard to find his son. On Tuesday, December 11, three months after the tragedy, Jonathan Ielpi's body was discovered and left where it lay until Lee arrived, knelt down, and lovingly picked up his son and carried him away.

Lee Ielpi never gave up. That's a father's love—it never, ever, ever, ever gives up. Lee's love for his son was greater than the pain of the search.

When I think of Jesus in the garden those final hours and wonder how he persevered to the end, I think of his great love for us. I think of love that endures. Why didn't he quit? Because his love for you and me was much greater than the pain of the search.

Jesus has come to pull you out. Your world has collapsed, and you are dead in your sin. There is no way you are getting out of this on your own. He relentlessly and lovingly pursues you. He loves you. That's why he never quits.

Love endures all things.

Love never fails.

Sunday Reflection:
Garden of Gethsemane

Read Matthew 26:36–46.

1. Why do you think Jesus took the disciples to the garden?

2. What did Jesus experience in his prayer that was so distressing?

3. What can we learn from Jesus about our own distress?

4. What was the significance of the olive tree in the Holy of Holies?

5. What does it mean that Jesus said to the Lord God, "Not my will, but yours?"

Week Five: Garden of Gethsemane

Week Six: Arrest and Trial

John 18:1–19:15

Day 30: Identity

When he had finished praying, Jesus left with his disciples and crossed the Kidron Valley. On the other side there was a garden, and he and his disciples went into it. Now Judas, who betrayed him, knew the place, because Jesus had often met there with his disciples. So Judas came to the garden, guiding a detachment of soldiers and some officials from the chief priests and the Pharisees. They were carrying torches, lanterns, and weapons. Jesus, knowing all that was going to happen to him, went out and asked them, "Who is it you want?" "Jesus of Nazareth," they replied. "I am he," Jesus said. (And Judas the traitor was standing there with them.) When Jesus said, "I am he," they drew back and fell to the ground. Again he asked them, "Who is it you want?" "Jesus of Nazareth," they said. Jesus answered, "I told you that I am he. If you are looking for me, then let these

*men go." This happened so that the words
he had spoken would be fulfilled: "I have not
lost one of those you gave me." Then Simon
Peter, who had a sword, drew it and struck
the high priest's servant, cutting off his right
ear. (The servant's name was Malchus.) Jesus
commanded Peter, "Put your sword away!
Shall I not drink the cup the Father has given
me?"* (John 18:1–11)

One of the defining moments of my life was when I
moved from my childhood home in Bethany, Oklahoma,
to attend Baylor University in Waco, Texas. As my mom
hugged me goodbye that day, she said, "Son, don't ever
forget where you came from." She wanted to remind me
of something that is actually very powerful in the human
heart—our identity, which carries our sense of person-
hood and significance.

Having an identity allows us to stand out as individuals
and develop well-being and importance; it is what helps
us fit into the world around us. Our identity gives us
strength to stand for our values and to establish our path
to the future. Without an identity, people tend to drift. If
we don't know who we are, then we are vulnerable to
allowing others to tell us who we are.

Jesus faced the darkest and most challenging hour of

his life when he stood in the garden with the disciples waiting for the temple guards to arrest him. When they asked him if he was Jesus of Nazareth, his answer was powerfully significant:

"I am he!" Jesus said.

The actual literal translation is "I AM!" Jesus used the identifying characteristic of God himself, the name the Lord God used to identify himself in Exodus 3:13–15:

> *Then Moses said to God, "If I come to the people of Israel and say to them, 'The God of your fathers has sent me to you,' and they ask me, 'What is his name?' what shall I say to them?" God said to Moses, "I AM WHO I AM." And he said, "Say this to the people of Israel, 'I AM has sent me to you.'" God also said to Moses, "Say this to the people of Israel, 'The Lord, the God of your fathers, the God of Abraham, the God of Isaac, and the God of Jacob, has sent me to you.' This is my name forever, and thus I am to be remembered throughout all generations."*

What is the meaning of "I AM WHO I AM?" The most common name for God in the Old Testament is "Yahweh," often translated as THE LORD. The name

Yahweh and the name I AM are built from the same Hebrew word, hayah. Interestingly, in this passage the word, Yahweh, seems to be used interchangeably with I AM: Verse 14 says "I AM has sent me to you" and verse 15, "Yahweh … has sent me to you."

By using this expression, God revealed the meaning of his personal name, Yahweh, to Moses. The key is in the phrase, I AM, and especially in the phrase, I AM WHO I AM, which carries some significant characteristics of God that are important to understand.

First, I AM WHO I AM means God exists, an important place to start because many people treat God as if he were not there at all. What if you were invited to have lunch with the CEO of your company, but during the entire lunch you never acknowledged his presence? How do you think that would go over? But that is exactly how many people treat God: as if he were not real or were some unseen substance like hydrogen. They may say God surrounds them, but he is not someone to whom they can relate. When God said, "I AM," he meant that he exists, and he can relate to us.

Second, I AM WHO I AM means nothing existed before God, and before anything was created, God existed. God is the uncaused cause. Nothing created God or was before God. All that we have, all that we are, and all that we ever will be is because of the Lord God. He is our creator and sustainer.

Third, God's name means he never changes. Nothing in all the universe can move him or change his character. God is the unmoved mover who foresees everything that happens in life, and by his unlimited source of energy and power, God makes all things conform to his divine will. He is who he is, and therefore, as James says, "With him there is no variation or shadow due to change" (James 1:17). He is the same yesterday, today, and forever (Hebrews 13:8). He is the granite foundation of our confidence and strength.

So as you can see, when Jesus used the words "I AM," he made a powerfully profound announcement of his identity. It must have been utterly shocking to everyone who heard it. But I want you to think about an important connection between Jesus' statement of his true identity and the suffering he was about to endure:

It is essential that we know our true identity to get through the many challenges we face in life.

How could Jesus possibly take on the sins of the world by dying on that cruel Roman cross? How could he find the strength and stamina to endure to the end?

How could he sustain his determination while the Father turned his face away? How could he drink the horrible cup of wrath? How could he sustain the fiery blast from the furnace of God's eternal justice? The answer is that Jesus knew who he was. He knew where he came from and where he was going.

Similarly, you and I must know our true identity as we seek to accomplish God's purpose for our lives. Life will get hard. Life may at times seem unbearable. But if we know who we are and understand our true identity, we can do more than merely survive—we can thrive!

What is your identity? It is what you think of first when people say to you, "Tell me about yourself." When you peel back all the layers, what defines you as a person? Your answer to that question will reveal what is most significant in your life and where you get your identity. But here is one of the most important themes of the Scriptures: If you get your identity from anything other than God's purposes, your life will inevitably become overwhelming.

If you get your identity from your career, one day it will disappoint you. If you get your sense of worth from your family, your personality, your status, your money, or anything else that is not God, those things will ultimately devastate you because they are only temporary. It is important that you get your identity from the one thing that can never be taken away from you—the fact that God loves you and was willing to die on the cross for you. That is the most important thing about you. That is your identity.

So when you look at yourself in the mirror and ask, "Who am I?" your answer should begin with God's pronouncement in the garden the day of Jesus' arrest and eventual sacrificial death on the cross for your sins:

I am loved!

Day 31: Security

Jesus answered, "I told you that I am he. If you are looking for me, then let these men go." This happened so that the words he had spoken would be fulfilled: "I have not lost one of those you gave me" (John 18:8–9).

There is no pain like rejection. Some people who experience profound rejection in their lives never get over it. I know a highly successful businessman whose father rejected him when he was a child, and who has spent a lifetime trying to make up for the hurt. His work-aholism stems from this early rejection. Everyone experiences some form of rejection, perhaps from a friend, a family member, a job, a school, or a lover. The pain is difficult because it feels personal, and begs the question, "What is wrong with me?"

But there is one person who will never reject you, and that is Jesus.

The Bible teaches that once you have come into his family, he will keep hold of you to the end:

> *For I am convinced that neither death nor life, neither angels nor demons, neither the present nor the future, nor any powers, neither height nor depth, nor anything else in all creation will be able to separate us from the love of God that is in Christ Jesus our Lord* (Romans 8:38–39).

Jesus protected his disciples from arrest to demonstrate that he will never fail us. He will keep us securely in his strong grip. *"I give them eternal life, and they shall never perish; no one will snatch them out of my hand,"* Jesus said in John 10:28.

This security is vital to our spiritual lives. We do not need to live in the fear of rejection because the one who knows us the best loves us the most and has promised to never let us go.

Rejection can lead to insecurity, which can create all kinds of other problems. When we feel insecure, we try to compensate in ways that are unhealthy to ourselves and others. Insecurity makes people do and say foolish things, which leads to more insecurity.

But when we deeply know the love of God, there is no reason to feel insecure. Jesus never stops loving us. Just like the disciples in the garden on the night of his arrest, Jesus will always have our backs. Nothing can separate us from his love. We may lose the things we have in this world, but we will never lose the love of Jesus.

Day 32: Surrender

Then Simon Peter, who had a sword, drew it and struck the high priest's servant, cutting off his right ear. (The servant's name was Malchus.) Jesus commanded Peter, "Put your sword away! Shall I not drink the cup the Father has given me?" (John 18:8–9)

You've gotta love Simon Peter. He's the first guy in the water. He's the one most likely to put his foot in his mouth. His enthusiasm for Jesus is infectious, and his love for him unquestioned. So when Jesus is about to be arrested by the temple guard, we could almost predict he would be the one to draw the sword.

Maybe the reason we love the Apostle Peter so much is because he reminds us of ourselves. We are all guilty of wanting to give Jesus a little help every now and then, are we not? Obviously, Peter thought, "Jesus can't handle this situation on his own, so I will single-handedly scare away the temple guard plus the detachment of highly trained Roman soldiers with the little short sword I keep in my belt."

What would Jesus do without him?

Every single day , we must decide who is in control—Jesus or ourselves.

The choice is a constant struggle. There is so much we want to control. We want to take charge of the consequential issues that affect us and make them work out to our advantage. But one of the most important things any of us can learn is that much of our worry and stress is based on our desire to control those things that only God can control. When we learn to give God control, stress disappears. Start by saying, "God, I'm giving up control because you can control the things that are out of my control." The psalmist says:

> *Let go of your concerns! Then you will know that I am God. I rule the nations. I rule the earth* (Psalm 46:10 GW).

The key to coping with stress is to recognize that God rules the earth and to surrender to his control. There is nothing in this life that he does not know or understand. God is not surprised by your problems. God knows every detail of your life and sees your past, present, and future all at once. He is working out all things for the good of those who are called according to his purpose (Romans 8:28). The Bible teaches that for the Christ follower, the truly bad things in this life will be turned to good, the truly good things cannot be taken away, and the very best is yet to come! That is the reality you and I live with as believers.

Jesus was in control of the situation in the garden. He was not surprised by the temple guard. He told the disciples they were coming and that he was in control. And yet Peter drew the sword anyway. Likewise, we have a tendency to take matters into our own hands. God has told us he is in control, and yet we want to take it on ourselves.

Whatever you are facing this week, let go and let God. Resist the temptation to try to control things that are not under your control. I am sure you have heard of the "Serenity Prayer" written by American theologian, Reinhold Niebuhr, in the 1930s. But maybe you have never read the original version in its entirety:

> *God, give me grace to accept with serenity*
> *the things that cannot be changed,*
> *Courage to change the things*
> *which should be changed,*
> *and the Wisdom to distinguish*

the one from the other.
Living one day at a time,
Enjoying one moment at a time,
Accepting hardship as a pathway to peace,
Taking, as Jesus did,
This sinful world as it is,
Not as I would have it,
Trusting that You will make all things right,
If I surrender to Your will,
So that I may be reasonably happy in this life,
And supremely happy with You forever in the next.

In 1936, a student of Niebuhr made the first published reference to this prayer, which grew in popularity throughout the 1940s, spreading from the eastern seaboard of the United States across the entire country. During World War II, the prayer was printed on cards and distributed to soldiers by the USO. After the war, Alcoholics Anonymous adopted it, and the lines are now quoted throughout the English-speaking world. I believe the reason for the prayer's popularity is that it resonates with the human heart—we want to control things we can't control. That was Peter's problem when he drew his sword, and it is our problem as well.

Our tendency is to go to one of two extremes when we face chaotic situations. Some of us "try harder." The more out of control we feel, the more desperately we seek to control every aspect of our lives. On the other extreme, some of us "give up." When life gets out of control, we retreat into a shell and throw a pity party—everyone is invited, but you are the only one who ever shows up!

Neither of these extremes is effective. Instead of becoming a control freak or playing the victim, we need to pray the prayer of surrender. Stress comes from conflict with God, when we try to control things only God can control. We can't control our spouses, our kids, our bosses, or our futures, and the more we try, the more we play God, which puts us in conflict with him. Only God can do God's job. If we try to do it, not only will we fail, but we also will burn out trying.

Peter's attempt to take control in the garden nearly ended in disaster before Jesus stepped in. He rebuked Peter and reminded him who was in control. We should not forget the lesson: When we try to play God, we just make a mess of things and stress ourselves out.

That's why we love Simon Peter—we have so much to learn from him!

Day 33: Injustice

Then the detachment of soldiers with its commander and the Jewish officials arrested Jesus. They bound him and brought him first to Annas, who was the father-in-law of Caiaphas, the high priest that year. Caiaphas was the one who had advised the Jewish leaders that it would be good if one man died for the people (John 18:12–15).

Then Pilate took Jesus and had him flogged. The soldiers twisted together a crown of thorns and put it on his head. They clothed him in a purple robe and went up to him again and again, saying, "Hail, king of the Jews!" And they slapped him in the face. Once more Pilate came out and said to the Jews gathered there, "Look, I am bringing him out to you to let you know that I find no basis for a charge against him." When Jesus came out wearing the crown of thorns and the purple

robe, Pilate said to them, "Here is the man!"
(John 19:1–5)

I had a business law professor in college who repeated the same four words every time we met for class: "Life is not fair." At the beginning of the semester he told us that if we remembered only one thing in his class, he wanted us to remember those four words. His fill-in-the-blank tests always included at least one question around those words: "Life is not _____" or sometimes, "_____ is not fair."

He was serious about our remembering those four words.

Indeed, after all these years, the only thing I remember about business law is those four words. In his opinion there was really nothing more important to learn than that one truth. You can't go around thinking life is fair because you will only become disillusioned.

Everyone knows life is not fair. But how do we know it? I think one of the best evidences for God's existence is the innate sense of fairness in every person. All of us, even the most hardened atheist, wants to live in a universe with a sense of justice and to understand unfairness when it raises its ugly head. But where do we get our understanding of fairness? Not from evolution or our

204   Week Six: Arrest and Trial

own goodness or righteousness. It can only come from outside ourselves, from God and his word. In Proverbs, we read the following:

> *The LORD detests differing weights, and dishonest scales do not please him* (Proverbs 20:23).

Justice is foundational to God's character (Psalm 89:14), and God does not approve of partiality, whether we are talking about a weighted scale or an unjust legal system (Leviticus 19:15). We find the issue of injustice throughout the Scriptures (2 Chronicles 19:7; Job 6:29; 11:14; Proverbs 16:8; Ezekiel 18:24; Romans 9:14).

Isaiah lived in a time when Judah was struggling under the weight of injustice:

> *Justice is driven back, and righteousness stands at a distance; truth has stumbled in the streets, honesty cannot enter. Truth is nowhere to be found, and whoever shuns evil becomes a prey. The LORD looked and was displeased that there was no justice* (Isaiah 59:14–15).

God's message for the people was simple:

Learn to do right; seek justice. Defend the oppressed. Take up the cause of the fatherless; plead the case of the widow (Isaiah 1:17).

Later, God says to "loose the chains of injustice" (Isaiah 58:6; Psalm 82:3), indicating that injustice is a form of bondage and oppression.

The book of James digs a little deeper into the issue of injustice, and we learn that the root cause of injustice is a lack of love. In chapter two, James speaks to a group of believers who have been playing favorites based on social status. Injustice is a sign of partiality, judgmental attitudes, and a lack of love. When we try to be righteous by our own human measurements, we invariably forget God's measurement: perfection. Anything less than perfection is, to God, a scale out of balance.

All of us are inherently unjust because of the sin that permeates our lives. We judge others unfairly and don't give them the same break we give ourselves. As James says, *"We all stumble in many ways"* (James 3:2). What is our solution?

Jesus came to resolve the world's injustice.

By every measure, the arrest and trial of Jesus was unjust. According to legal scholar and historian Steven

Steward, Jesus' arrest was illegal on at least three grounds of Hebrew law: It was a nighttime arrest; it was affected by Judas, who would have been considered an accomplice of Jesus; and it was not based on probable cause by officials seeking righteous judgment. According to first century Hebrew laws, either the trial should never have taken place, or at the very least, Jesus should have been acquitted based on multiple legal violations. And that was only according to the Hebrew laws.

When Jesus was handed over to Pilate, a whole new set of ethical problems ensued. Why did Jesus go before the Romans? The Jewish religious leaders wanted Pilate to execute Jesus because only the Romans had the right to execute on criminal charges. The Romans had removed the death penalty from the Jews' authority, and any criminal charge the Jews might bring would be subject to Pilate's approval or vetoed.

The Romans prided themselves in their sense of justice. As attorney Walter Chandler noted, "The Roman judicial system is incomparable in the history of jurisprudence. Judea gave religion, Greece gave letters, and Rome gave laws to mankind. Thus runs the judgment of the world."

And yet the Romans were also guilty of an unjust verdict. First of all, the charge of blasphemy would not have held up in a Roman court and certainly was not worthy of execution. Second, Pilate at first ruled that Jesus was "without fault," and then changed the verdict after pressure from the Jews. His action, called "double jeopardy" in the court, would have been a basis for acquittal. And yet, Jesus was sentenced to death and brutally executed.

No one in history was more unjustly sentenced than Jesus of Nazareth, but because of his great love and grace, Jesus endured the injustices of the Hebrew and Roman courts. He never lashed out. He remained calm, and even prayed for his accusers, asking God to forgive them because they "know not what they do" (Luke 23:34).

What does this mean for us? Because Jesus endured such injustice, he identifies with all injustice in the world in a very personal way:

> *For we do not have a high priest who is unable to empathize with our weaknesses, but we have one who has been tempted in every way, just as we are—yet he did not sin* (Hebrews 4:15).

Jesus took all of the world's injustice onto himself so that we could be shown mercy. He who knew no sin became sin for us, that we might become the righteousness of

God (2 Corinthians 5:21). And one day all of history will culminate in the ultimate day of justice in which God will make everything right. In *The Prodigal God*, Tim Keller wrote this:

> *Jesus hates suffering, injustice, evil, and death so much that he came and experienced it to defeat it and someday, to wipe the world clean of it. Knowing this, Christians cannot be passive about hunger, sickness, and injustice. Karl Marx and others have charged that religion is "the opiate of the masses." That is, it is a sedative that makes people passive towards injustice, because there will be "pie in the sky bye and bye." That may be true of some religions that teach people that this material world is unimportant or illusory. Christianity, however, teaches that God hates the suffering and oppression of this material world so much, that he was willing to get involved in it and to fight against it. Properly understood, Christianity is by no means the opiate of the people. It is more like the smelling salts.*

Truly, life is not fair. But because of what Jesus accomplished on the cross and what he will fulfill in the final judgment, all of life's unfairness will one day be overwhelmed within the scales of eternity. Only then will the innate sense of justice our hearts so desperately long for be fully and infinitely satisfied.

Day 34: Restoration

While Peter was below in the courtyard, one of the servant girls of the high priest came by. When she saw Peter warming himself, she looked closely at him. "You also were with that Nazarene, Jesus," she said. But he denied it. "I don't know or understand what you're talking about," he said, and went out into the entryway. When the servant girl saw him there, she said again to those standing around, "This fellow is one of them." Again he denied it. After a little while, those standing near said to Peter, "Surely you are one of them, for you are a Galilean." He began to call down curses, and he swore to them, "I don't know this man you're talking about." Immediately the rooster crowed the second time. Then Peter remembered the word Jesus had spoken to him: "Before the rooster crows twice you will disown me three times." And he broke down and wept (Mark 14:66-72).

When we become believers in Christ, we are secure in our salvation and nothing can take us from his hand. Our relationship with God is secure, although there will be times when our sin may impact our fellowship with him. Here is one of the wonderful truths of the Christian life: We are always only one step away from being completely restored in our relationship with God. The book of Jeremiah says:

> *If you return to Me, I will restore you so you can continue to serve me* (Jeremiah 15:19a NLT).

The Bible teaches that the only thing that we need to do to be completely reconciled in our relationship with God is to return to him and come back into the fellowship. It really is that simple. Isaiah, the prophet, said this to Israel, but it also applies to us:

> *No matter how deep the stain of your sins, I can take it out and make you as clean as freshly fallen snow* (Isaiah 1:18 LB).

Maybe today you believe you are so far from God that there is no way he would ever take you back. Maybe you think you are too much of a sinner, a lost cause. I talk to people all the time who tell me they are afraid to come to church because they think the roof might cave in. I tell them if it hasn't caved in already, it certainly won't now! The church is made up of sinners who are constantly reconciling to God. The church is more a hospital for sinners than a sanctuary for saints.

If there were ever a sin bad enough to cause the roof to cave in, it would have been denying Jesus three times on the night he was arrested. But Jesus not only knew Peter would be the one to deny him, he also knew that Peter would return to him. He said this to him in the Upper Room:

> *I have pleaded in prayer for you that your faith should not completely fail. So when you have repented and turned to me again, strengthen and build up the faith of your brothers* (Luke 22:32).

Those words are great encouragement to the person who needs to reconcile with God, and that includes all of us. Jesus knew that Peter's ministry would actually be better and more effective AFTER his denial than it had been before! Our mistakes can actually serve a divine purpose in God's eternal and sovereign plan. God never wastes a pain. We make our choices, and God redeems them. This fact was definitely true for Peter, who wrote two of the books of the Bible—1 and 2 Peter—and also was a big influence on the writing of the book of Mark.

Of course, we should not willingly rebel against God and take our sin lightly. The more we love Jesus, the more we want to please him, and the more our hearts are broken over sin. But the point is, we should not let our inevitable failures keep us from repentance and restoration.

So the next time you think you are too far from God or that God has forgotten you, remember what happened to Peter in the courtyard. At that low point, he must have wondered if his life would ever be restored to God's purposes. Yet, Peter became a dynamic leader in the emergence of the church.

The lesson is that God never gives up on us so we should never give up on our relationship with him. We are always only one step away from a restored relationship. The Good Shepherd leaves the ninety-nine sheep to seek the one. God has not forgotten you. He knows all about your rebellion, your mistakes, and your denials, and he will receive you back. I love this eighteenth-century hymn by Joseph Hart:

> *Come ye sinners, poor and needy*
> *Weak and wounded, sick and sore*
> *Jesus ready stands to save you*
> *Full of pity, love, and power*
>
> *Come ye thirsty, come and welcome*

God's free bounty glorify
True belief and true repentance
Every grace that brings you nigh

Come ye weary, heavy-laden
Lost and ruined by the fall
If you tarry until you're better
You will never come at all

I will arise and go to Jesus
He will embrace me in His arms
In the arms of my dear Savior
Oh, there are ten thousand charms.

Day 35: Responsibility

So when Pilate saw that he was gaining nothing, but rather that a riot was beginning, he took water and washed his hands before the crowd, saying, "I am innocent of this man's blood; see to it yourselves." And all the people answered, "His blood be on us and on our children!" Then he released for them Barabbas, and having scourged Jesus, delivered him to be crucified (Matthew 27:24–26).

Some people don't want to take responsibility for their bad choices. *"Do not be deceived: God cannot be mocked. A man reaps what he sows,"* the Bible says in Galatians 6:7. My dad used to say, "You can't sow wild oats and then pray for a crop failure!" The choices we make in life have consequences, and therefore, we must take responsibility for them regardless of how they turn out. I have learned that there are basically three ways to respond to bad choices: accusing, excusing, or choosing.

Sometimes we respond by accusing others. We don't want to admit we could make such a bad choice, and so we deflect the choice onto someone else. This is what Adam did in the Garden of Eden when he told God, *"It was the woman you gave me, Lord!"* (Genesis 3:12) Once when our kids were very young, I watched my son throw a toy at his little sister. As she burst into tears, he immediately looked at me and said, "I didn't do that!"

How crazily innate is our tendency to deflect bad choices! My son was barely old enough to have self-awareness, and he was already making excuses for his hurtful decisions. That is how we are: We find it hard to believe we are capable of doing bad things on our own, and as a way of coping, we impulsively accuse others.

Another way we rationalize our bad choices is to make excuses. Excuse-making is the result of fear. We fear failure; we fear embarrassment; we fear what people might think about us. Sometimes we fear the truth.

Years ago while on vacation, my family narrowly missed a head-on collision in Yuma, Arizona. An elderly couple was driving on the wrong side of I-40 at about seventy miles per hour and drove us off the interstate. The highway patrol caught up to them and brought them back to our car. The elderly woman looked at me and said to the officer, "Well, we may have been on the wrong side of the road, but he was driving too fast!"

My first thought was, "I'm in Yuma, Arizona, hundreds of miles from my church in Texas, I can say what I want to this woman." But I denied the impulse and said instead, "Ma'am, when you are driving seventy miles per hour in the wrong lane, everyone is driving too fast!"

I could see the fear on this poor woman's face. The truth about her terrible driving was too hard for her to bear at that moment, and so she impulsively accused others. Her response was natural to fear.

Our best response to mistakes is to take responsibility, instead of excusing our behavior or accusing others for our mistakes. When we own up to our bad choices, we start down the road to healing and learning. Taking responsibility when we hurt people also helps to heal the relationship. And the only way to truly learn from mistakes is to own them, because how can we learn from mistakes we never admit to having made?

In the account of Jesus' sentencing in Matthew 27, Pilate made excuses for his tragic choice. The cliché, "I wash my hands of that decision," is an excuse we make that harkens back to the story of Jesus' trial. Pilate refused to own up to his choice and to take responsibility.

But what about Jesus? Look at Jesus standing before Pilate, blood streaming down his face from the crown of thorns and bruises all over his body. Jesus made no excuses, nor did he accuse. Jesus took the responsibility for all the bad choices and sins of all humanity for all time onto himself in that moment. For his followers, Jesus is the supreme example of taking responsibility. The first Adam made excuses and accused others for his bad choices. The second Adam chose to take responsibility for things that were not his fault. The Bible says:

> *We are each responsible for our own conduct* (Galatians 6:5 NLT).

Instead of complaining that you haven't achieved what you want from life, follow Jesus' example and take responsibility for what hasn't been done. Your good and bad choices and how you heal and learn from them have a far greater impact on your future than any other factor.

I've met people who were given nothing in life but achieved far beyond their wildest dreams. I've also met people who had everything they needed and wanted on a silver platter and yet wasted their lives by making excuses and accusing others.

You can't control your circumstances, but you can control the choices you make in those circumstances.

Don't accuse, don't make excuses, choose to take responsibility.

Sunday Reflection:
Arrest and Trial

Read John 18:1–19:15

1. In what ways was the arrest of Jesus unjust?

2. What does our sense of justice say about the existence of God?

3. Why was Jesus a threat to religious leaders?

4. What does the example of Pilate teach us about making bad choices?

5. How does Jesus respond to injustice?

Week Six: Arrest and Trial

Passion Week: Agony

Matthew 27:32–56

Day 36: Spectacle

There they crucified him, and with him two others—one on each side and Jesus in the middle (John 19:18).

In 71 B.C., a slave named Spartacus led a revolt against the Romans that eventually was decimated. The Romans captured approximately 6,000 slaves and crucified them at varying distances for 119 miles along the Appian Highway between Rome and Capua. The display was gruesomely effective at sending an unmistakable message.

In the same way, Jesus was crucified on a hill just outside of Jerusalem along with two criminals, where passersby could see their broken bodies. Crucifixion was not just a form of punishment; it also demonstrated what would happen to anyone who dared to challenge the power of the Roman Empire. The cross was an instrument of torture as well as a powerful and unforgettable

224

spectacle meant to be wrathful, horrifically cruel, and vividly picturesque. In *King's Cross*, Tim Keller wrote:

> *Crucifixion was designed to be the most humiliating and gruesome method of execution. The Romans reserved it for their worst offenders. It was a protracted, bloody public spectacle of extreme pain that usually ended in a horrible death by shock or asphyxiation.*

But death on a wooden beam was only the final part of the torture. Prior to taking up the cross, there was flogging, beating, beard-pulling, spitting, and finally cross-carrying and naked humiliation. Once Jesus arrived at the place of execution, his hands and feet were nailed to the beams, and the cross was hoisted into a deep hole to keep it upright for the duration of his suffering. It was uncensored cruelty on an inhuman scale and a picture of the grotesque nature of man's depravity and sinful condition.

Crucifixion was meant to look ugly, an execution of criminals and insurrectionists, violent, degenerate people who had no regard for life or laws. The cross was for rebels and murderers like Barabbas or slaves who led revolts like Spartacus. It was for sinners, law violators, rebels, and reprobates.

Not only did Jesus die in our place as a substitute for our sin, but he also was publicly executed as a heinous criminal with the most disgusting and wrathful punishment in human history. Jesus did not die in private. He did not die quietly. He was lifted up publicly between heaven and earth, and the abject ugliness of his agony and suffering was on full display.

God wanted us to see it. He wanted us to see the ugliness of our sin. He wanted us to see the horrible consequences of our fallenness. He wanted human depravity in all of its horrible defilement to be seen in living color. He wanted us to see what we all deserved, but Christ absorbed.

Maybe you are thinking right now that you don't want to see it. You want to look away. Maybe the idea of Jesus being crucified is too much for you to think about—all that violence and blood and suffering. But Mary watched. She wanted to see the cruel death of her son for herself. Her love for Jesus compelled her to watch. And for the very same reason, God wants you to behold his cruel death. He wants you to see it for what it is. He wants you to go all the way with him to the cross so that you can understand.

Here is the profound truth: If we do not see him suspended on that cross between heaven and earth, we lose the picture of redemption; we lose the significance of God's perfect justice and righteousness poured out on an innocent man who by his death atoned for the devastating rebellion at the center of every human heart. With the crucifixion, God says, "Here is what horror your sin brings, and here is how much I love you to atone for it!"

This is why Christians say the worst thing that ever happened in history was also the best thing that ever happened. There on the cross, we see the intersection of God's great sense of justice and his incomparable love and mercy.

Do not turn away from the spectacle of the cross. Look at it with sorrow and horror, for that is what your sin accomplishes. But also, look at it with great joy and thankfulness, for there is the incredible love of God on full display.

> *And I, when I am lifted up from the earth, will draw all people to myself* (John 12:32).

Day 37: Redemption

For our sake, he made him to be sin who knew no sin, so that in him we might become the righteousness of God (2 Corinthians 5:21 ESV).

Why did Jesus have to die? That is a question I have heard many times through the years. If God is all powerful, then why couldn't he just wave a magic wand and forgive everyone? It seems extreme on a grand scale that the Son of God would have to die for our sin. The idea that Jesus would die in our place seems absurd to many modern people. After all, we forgive people all the time. People ask our forgiveness and we say, "No big deal—you're forgiven!" It seems easy enough. Why can't God just let sin go?

There are two important answers to this question. First, God doesn't just "let sin go" because he is God. God is not like us. We forgive people all the time and move on. But God exists in perfect righteousness and holiness, and therefore, he can't just ignore sin. If we think about it, we really wouldn't want it any other way. None of us wants to live in a universe without a righteous and holy God. We all want justice. We all want to know there is fairness, moral goodness, and order to our existence. Otherwise, it would be "anything goes" and only the strong would survive. There would be nothing wrong with rape, murder, exploitation, and genocide. God doesn't "let sin go" because God is holy, and ignoring unrighteousness and sin is not in his nature.

Second, all forgiveness costs something. No one who has ever been deeply wronged "just forgives and moves on." There is always a price to pay. If someone sins against you, you can either make the sinner pay in some way, or you can forgive and pay the price.

Suppose someone comes to your home and accidentally breaks your lamp. You can forgive and say, "Don't worry; I didn't like that old lamp anyway," and then absorb the cost yourself. Or, you can say, "You owe me a lamp!" in which case the offender absorbs the cost. We cannot forgive without paying some kind of price, no matter how big or small; therefore, how much more must God absorb the cost to forgive us? Cosmic sin requires cosmic payment.

If we can instinctively sense an obligation of the debt

of forgiveness and justice in our own fallen hearts, how much more does God, in his perfect sense of holiness and righteousness, sense it? On the cross we see the cost of God's forgiveness on full display: God had to suffer to bring about forgiveness, bearing the price for our sinful condition. There is NEVER forgiveness without a price being paid. And for God that price meant nails, thorns, sweat, tears, blood. He took the blow for sin so we wouldn't have to. He absorbed the cost so that we could be forgiven. He drank the cup of wrath so we could drink the cup of blessing. He put on eternal death so we could put on eternal life.

He took the tree of death so we could have the tree of life.

Day 38: Gospel

Fellow Israelites, listen to this: Jesus of Nazareth was a man accredited by God to you by miracles, wonders and signs, which God did among you through him, as you yourselves know. This man was handed over to you by God's deliberate plan and foreknowledge; and you, with the help of wicked men, put him to death by nailing him to the cross (Acts 2:22–23).

The word "gospel" means "good news." And that good news can be summarized in one sentence:

Your sin is so cosmically bad, the God of the universe had to die to pay the price for it, but God's love for you is so profoundly deep, he was willing to die!

Actually, the Gospel is both really BAD news and

really GOOD news simultaneously.

The Greek word for gospel, which is transliterated as euaggelion, has a fascinating history that will help us understand its significance. In ancient Greek cities, the only method for widely distributing information was through specially assigned heralds who would shout news from a pedestal in the city center. Think of the "town crier" in colonial America. Heralds would proclaim news that was sometimes insignificant, like the price of barley and wheat, or the latest gossip.

But they also occasionally proclaimed information that was extremely significant, like news of a battle that would determine the fate of the city. A military defeat could mean absolute devastation, or rape, murder, and slavery for a city's inhabitants. Thus, at times the entire city would rush to the town square to hear the news from the herald because their very existence depended on that news. Bad news meant devastation and the loss of everything precious. Good news (euagglelion) meant salvation and rejoicing.

The most famous example in Greek history of a messenger who heralded good news is the story of Phillipedes, the Athenian soldier who ran 26.2 miles from Marathon to Athens to inform the city that their army had defeated the invading Persians, and the city was saved. His announcement was life-changing news to the Athenians. It was euagglelion.

Thus, we see that this word is packed with meaning, which is what the Gospel should mean to each of us— life-changing news.

On our way to the cross, I think it is important to meditate on one important aspect of the Gospel, the fact that God was WILLING to die for us. His sacrifice was intentional, and it is no exaggeration to say that the execution of Jesus Christ was the greatest injustice in history. Jesus was the only human being who ever lived who was without sin, and yet he was ruthlessly crucified on a cruel Roman cross.

But that is not the end of the story. The crucifixion was also the greatest act of divine justice in human history, an act done "with the determined purpose and foreknowledge of God" (Acts 2:23). Think of it this way: By his death, Jesus Christ willingly secured the salvation of all who come to him, and he opened the way for God to forgive sin without compromising his perfect sense of righteousness and justice. The Bible says:

> *When they hurled their insults at him, he did not retaliate; when he suffered, he made no threats. Instead, he entrusted himself*

*to him who judges justly. He himself bore
our sins in his body on the cross, so that
we might die to sins and live for righteousness; by his wounds you have been healed*
(1 Peter 2:23–24).

The story of the cross is not simply that Jesus was
crucified unjustly by men with evil intent. The full story
is much more significant than that. Christ died intention-
ally as an atonement for the sins of the unjust. Not only
was Jesus' execution on the cross the greatest injustice,
it also was the greatest willing sacrifice, the purest act
of mercy and love. Ultimately, Christ's death was an
infinitely greater act of divine justice than all the world's
injustices. The true reality of the cross is the greatest
truth overshadowing every other reality: God loves you
enough to die for you. Your life, and all human life, has
incredible value. Your sins are forgiven and forgotten,
the enemy defeated, and your salvation secured. Now
you will spend eternity with him. That reality is the most
important truth about you!

The profound nature of God's love is not just that
he loves the whole world all at once, but that he loves
everyone in the world as if each person were the only
one to love. That is why the Gospel is called "good
news"—there is no other news that comes even close.

All believers know Jesus died for our sins, but do we know the full significance of that act? We could spend a thousand lifetimes diving into the depths of that profound truth. Do we take it for granted? I see many people wearing crosses around their necks as fashion statements, but I doubt many truly understand the unbelievable, spectacular statement the cross actually makes.

Look into the night sky, and you see millions of stars, but the second that dawn breaks, all those points of light are overwhelmed by the brightness of the sun. Like the morning sun that overwhelms the stars, the truth of the cross should outshine all other truths. It is the reality that outshines every other reality. C. S. Lewis said it best in *Mere Christianity*:

> *Christianity, if false, is of no importance, and if true, of infinite importance. The only thing Christianity cannot be is moderately important.*

We mistakenly think of the cross as just one of the elemental facts of our faith, but it is so much more. The cross is a lens through which we should see all of life. Jesus Christ was not a mere victim of human injustice, his death was God's plan all along. Far from being an example of tragic injustice, his death was the high point of God's eternal plan for redemption, the most incredible act of both divine justice and divine grace at the same instant.

This is the Gospel, and it is not moderately important news, but ultimately important, life-changing, life-shaping good news!

Day 39: Agony

About three in the afternoon Jesus cried out in a loud voice, "Eli, Eli, lema sabachthani?" (which means "My God, my God, why have you forsaken me?") (Mathew 27:46).

Jesus screamed.

The words translated "cried out in a loud voice" in this verse literally mean "screeched," but English translators used "cried out" because it sounds more civil. The Greek uses a more guttural expression. Someone reading this account for the first time in the original language may have thought Jesus was losing his mind.

But Jesus was not losing his mind because he was quoting Scripture. At the height of his suffering, when most of us in his place would be crying for mercy or cursing our tormentors, Jesus quoted the Psalms. He quoted Scripture as if it were the natural expression of his heart. Or rather, he screamed Scripture.

In his torment, Jesus quoted the first verse of Psalm 22, a psalter of David. Shockingly, King David describes in this particular Psalm the suffering of a Roman-style crucifixion, although he never experienced such torture. In fact, crucifixion would not exist as a means of execution for another 800 years. There was never a time when David's hands and feet were pierced and his bones were pulled out of joint. And yet that is exactly what he describes:

> *My God, my God, why have you forsaken me?*
> *Why are you so far from saving me,*
> *so far from my cries of anguish?*
> *My God, I cry out by day, but you do not answer,*
> *by night, but I find no rest...*
> *I am poured out like water,*
> *and all my bones are out of joint.*
> *My mouth is dried up like a potsherd,*
> *and my tongue sticks to the roof of my mouth;*
> *you lay me in the dust of death.*
> *Dogs surround me,*
> *a pack of villains encircles me;*
> *they pierce my hands and my feet.*
> *All my bones are on display;*
> *people stare and gloat over me.*
> *They divide my clothes among them*
> *and cast lots for my garment.*
> (Psalm 22 various)

At the most excruciating moment of Jesus' execution, why would he quote from Psalm 22? Clearly, this Psalm is a prophecy of Jesus' crucifixion. David's words are his words, but through the Holy Spirit, they are actually the thoughts of Jesus. How remarkable that Psalm 22 actually gives us insight into the mind of Jesus at the time of his suffering.

Tim Keller once observed that Jesus screamed, "My God, my God," not "My head, my head!" or "My hands, my hands!" He didn't say, "My side, my side!" Although he wore a crown of thorns, his hands and feet were pierced, and his side was stabbed, Jesus cried out, "My God, my God!"

Jesus' exclamation from the cross shows us that his greatest anguish was not physical pain, but the devastating spiritual loss of fellowship with the Father. For the first time in eternity, Father and Son were separated. At that moment, even God, the Father, had to turn away as Jesus bore the curse and identified himself with the sins of fallen humanity. He took upon himself the horror of hell for every person who ever lived or ever will live. He absorbed cosmic separation and death at an infinite level.

Psychologists tell us that the most painful experience we endure is the loss of love. If you said to me, "I never want to see you again," I probably would be hurt, but if my wife made that statement, I would be devastated. The agony of losing a relationship is directly proportional to the depth of the relationship. And the relationship between Father and Son was of cosmic proportion, and therefore, its loss was an agony we cannot even begin to understand or explain. No one ever experienced agony like what the Son of God experienced on the cross in that moment.

And that is why Jesus screamed.

Day 40: Darkness

From noon until three in the afternoon darkness came over all the land. And when Jesus had cried out again in a loud voice, he gave up his spirit. At that moment the curtain of the temple was torn in two from top to bottom. The earth shook, the rocks split and the tombs broke open (Matthew 27:45; 50–52).

Darkness descended as Jesus died. Some have said it must have been a sand storm, but sand storms don't happen in Jerusalem during the rainy season. Some have said it was an eclipse, but eclipses don't cause total darkness. The only possible explanation is that the darkness was a supernatural event in which God communicated something very important to all humanity: Life without God's love and grace is spiritual darkness.

Darkness carries important spiritual themes. It can denote sin and spiritual blindness, death, and loss of hope (See 2 Corinthians 4:4).

Physically, the human body cannot handle long periods of darkness. A unique experiment in 1965 demonstrated this effect. Two cave explorers, Josie Laures and Antoine Senni, volunteered to help scientists understand what happens to the human body over time when in utter darkness. They descended into the depths of a dark cave in the French Alps near the city of Nice and stayed there without any light for over three months. Without even the company of one another, they resided in separate caves a few hundred yards apart. They discovered that the mind begins to unhinge when in total darkness too long. The men lost track of sleep patterns, sometimes sleeping up to forty-eight hours at a time. Desperate for company, they compensated by making friends with rats they lured with honey. As their senses began shutting down, they became disoriented and depressed (*"The Caves of Forgotten Time," Atlantic Magazine*, November 19, 2015).

City folks don't know what real darkness looks like. Even those who live outside cities are not far from towns with bright lights. But true darkness is something altogether different. In such deep darkness you can't see in front of you, so you don't know where you're going. You have no sense of direction. You don't know up or down or right or left. You can't even see yourself; you don't know what you look like. You may as well have no identity. Without perspective of surrounding context, your sense of self becomes distorted. You are isolated with no sense of place.

Physical darkness brings disorientation, but according to the Bible, so does spiritual darkness. Spiritual darkness comes when we turn away from God as our true light and make something else the center of our hearts. The Bible describes God as being like the sun:

> *For the LORD God is a sun and shield; the LORD bestows favor and honor; no good thing does he withhold from those whose walk is blameless* (Psalm 84:11).

God is our true light and life. When we put our lives in the orbit of God's purposes, we see clearly and enjoy a sense of his presence and glory. But when we put other things at the center of our hearts, like money, career, status, or family, we spin out into a kind of spiritual darkness. Those things may give us a sense of purpose for a while, but eventually we become disoriented and lose direction.

None of us knows what it is like to live even one second in the absence of God's sustaining light. Even people who are far from God enjoy his grace in a general way. The righteous and unrighteous alike enjoy the warmth of the sun, the beauty of friendship, and the joy of love. These things are in our lives because God bestows his general grace on all humankind. But when God's grace is removed, there is utter darkness.

The earth must have experienced something like utter darkness in those three hours of Jesus' crucifixion. It must have been terrifying. But that's not all that happened. The Bible says that when Jesus breathed his last, the curtain in the temple was torn in two from top to bottom. This curtain was not something flimsy we might have covering our windows, but something big and thick— more like a wall. It was the barrier that kept people from entering the presence of Almighty God in the Holy of Holies. Only the High Priest could enter through the curtain, and then only after making elaborate sacrifices and cleansings once a year during Yom Kippur.

The moment Jesus died, the thick curtain was ripped from the top down, so that no one would have any doubts about who was responsible. This act was God's way of saying, "Now the barrier between my presence and my people has been removed forever!"

The disciples would come to understand these events only after they had time to reflect on Jesus' resurrection.

At the time of his death, after hours of darkness and earthquakes and the horrible spectacle of the bloody cross, they must have wondered if the cross had any meaning at all. All was darkness, hateful violence, fear, and confusion. But they would come to understand that the cross was the most important reality in their lives; and so can we.

Why is the cross important? Because it is the most consequential act of love, justice, and grace in the history of humanity. Jesus died on that cruel cross to save us from our sin. His death was the ultimate act of sacrifice, an act accomplished for you and me as the ultimate proof of his love.

There will be times in your life when you will suffer. And in those moments you may ask yourself, "Where is God?" or maybe you will even question if God cares at all. Whatever the answer to your painful experience might be, what will never be true is that God does not identify with your suffering or does not love you. God has proven for all time by his death on a Roman cross that he both knows and cares. You may not understand your suffering, just like the disciples did not understand why Jesus went to the cross, but when you consider the suffering of the cross and understand what Jesus came to accomplish, all your doubts about his love and purpose melt away.

Because of Jesus, darkness is a passing shadow. The only darkness that could have destroyed you forever fell into his heart at the moment he took his last breath. He died the death that you should have died so that you could live the life only he could live.

That is the most important truth about you. And it is the most important lesson we can learn on our way to the cross.

> *In him was life, and that life was the light of all mankind. The light shines in the darkness, and the darkness has not overcome it* (John 1:5).

Epilogue

Where, O death, is your victory? Where, O death, is your sting? The sting of death is sin, and the power of sin is the law. But thanks be to God! He gives us the victory through our Lord Jesus Christ (1 Corinthians 15:55–56).

I've never been afraid of spiders, but the spider that stalked me and my wife one night in the southern Jordanian desert near the historic Showback Castle gave me the creeps. It was the diameter of a small Frisbee with the fuzzy legs and fangs of something out of a horror movie. As we walked down the dark path, flashlights in hand, that spider moved with our every step. When we moved, it moved. When we stopped, it stopped. I had that weird sensation we were being followed, and as I shined my light off the path into the brush, there it was, staring at me with its beady eyes and long fangs.

When we made it back to our camp, I asked our

Jordanian hosts if they knew what kind of sadistic spider it was. "Oh yeah," they said, "that's a camel spider. Don't get stung by that! Its venom turns muscle into mush. Camel spiders have been known to cause U.S. soldiers in Iraq to lose arms or legs."

Sorry I asked.

Needless to say, we didn't sleep much after that. My wife zipped up our tent so tight that not even an oxygen molecule could squeeze through. From that point forward, we were constantly on the lookout for the nasty arachnid. A spider had struck fear into our hearts for the rest of the trip.

Later, I learned some fun facts about the camel spider. For instance, it's not really a spider at all, but a scorpion that only looks like a spider. Its actual name is "Egyptian giant solpugid," which makes the creature seem so much more warm and fuzzy. With the ability to move up to ten miles per hour, the camel spider is every desert insect and small rodent's nightmare. It also is attracted to light, which explains why it was following my flashlight.

I also discovered it is harmless to humans, unless you count dying from heart failure because of its inflated reputation. In fact, the giant solpugid doesn't even have venom—only a bite. That bite hurts like the dickens, and you will definitely know you've been bitten, but that's all. No swelling, no mushy muscles. Just a friendly reminder to "stay away from me, you nasty human."

In other words, my wife and I had spent the last few days of our Jordanian camping trip fearing something that didn't even exist. And that is exactly what Paul the Apostle said about our fear of death. In fact, in the original language, the word for "sting" is actually the word "venom." I wonder if Paul was referring to the notorious camel spider! Undoubtedly, he was familiar with its inflated reputation in and around Jerusalem and the Judean desert.

Where, oh Camel Spider, is your venom?
Where, oh Egyptian giant solpugid, is your sting?

Even in ancient times, nasty rumors persisted about camel spiders, which were thought to run as fast as humans and to eat small children. Although they look like they have venom and can pack a punch, they are not as bad as you think. That is Paul's lesson about death: Because of Jesus's death on the cross and his resurrection from the grave, death and sin have been defeated, and the venom has been taken away.

Because of Jesus, not even death can kill you. Death has been swallowed up in victory because of the resurrection of Jesus! Death may look bad, might even terrify you, but because of Jesus' victory, death has no power, no sting, no venom. Every Christian can look death in the face and say confidently, "Bring it on death, bring it on grave! The lower you lay me the higher he'll raise me!"

Praise be to God!

Recently our church hosted Irish singers and song writers, Keith and Kristyn Getty, for a night of praise. As long as I live, I will never forget our congregation singing with them their famous hymn, "In Christ Alone." I doubt anyone who was there will ever forget it either. As I write this and meditate on the words of 1 Corinthians 15, the last two verses of that song are lodged in my memory. I can think of no better way to finish our journey on the way to the cross than to consider these words:

> *There in the ground His body lay,*
> *Light of the world by darkness slain;*
> *Then bursting forth in glorious day,*
> *Up from the grave He rose again!*
> *And as He stands in victory,*
> *Sin's curse has lost its grip on me;*
> *For I am His and He is mine—*
> *Bought with the precious blood of Christ.*

No guilt in life, no fear in death—
This is the pow'r of Christ in me;
From life's first cry to final breath,
Jesus commands my destiny.
No pow'r of hell, no scheme of man,
Can ever pluck me from His hand;
Till He returns or calls me home—
Here in the pow'r of Christ I'll stand."

Bibliography

Carson, D. A. *Scandalous: The Cross and Resurrection of Jesus*. (Wheaton, IL: Crossway, 2010).

Keller, Tim. *Jesus the King, Understanding the Life and Death of the Son of God*. (New York: Penguin Books, 2013).

Leahy, Frederick S. *The Cross He Bore, The Victory of the Lamb, and Is It Nothing to You?* (Edinburgh: Banner of Truth, 1996, 2001, and 2004).

Mahaney, C. J. *Living the Cross-Centered Life* (New York: Multnomah Publishing, 2009).

Morris, Leon. *The Atonement: Its Meaning and Significance* (Leicester, England: Inter-Varsity Press, 1983).

Murray, John. *Redemption Accomplished and Applied* (Grand Rapids, MI: Eerdmans, 1955).

Packer, J.I., and Mark Dever. *In My Place Condemned He Stood: Celebrating the Glory of the Atonement* (Wheaton, IL: Crossway, 2008).

Pink, Arthur W. *The Seven Sayings of the Savior on the Cross* (Eastford, CT: Martino Fine Books, 2011).

Piper, John. *Fifty Reasons Why Jesus Came to Die* (Wheaton, IL: Crossway, 2006).

Ryken, Philip Graham, and James Montgomery Boice. *The Heart of the Cross* (Wheaton, IL: Crossway, 2005).

Sproul, R. C. *The Truth of the Cross.* (London: Reformation Publishing, 2007).

Stott, John R. W. *The Cross of Christ* (Leicester, England: Inter-Varsity Press, 1986).